Aristo

Patric

THE WAY OF THE CHRISTIAN MYSTICS

GENERAL EDITOR
Noel Dermot O'Donoghue, ODC

Volume 1

Aristocracy of Soul
Patrick of Ireland

by

Noel Dermot O'Donoghue, O.D.C.

Michael Glazier
Wilmington, Delaware

About the Author

Noel Dermot O'Donoghue, O.D.C., is a teaching member of
the Faculty of Divinity of the University of Edinburg, being
the first Catholic to obtain a full teaching post in a Scottish
Faculty of Theology since the Reformation. He has a doc-
torate in philosophy from the University of Louvain. He has
published about a hundred articles in various scholarly, pastoral and spiritual journals, and a collection of these articles
in a book entitled *Heaven in Ordinaire*. Among his other
books is included: *The Holy Mountain: Approaches to the
Mystery of Prayer.*

First published in 1987 by Michael Glazier, Inc. 1935 West Fourth
Street, Wilmington, Delaware, 19805. ©1987 by Michael Glazier, Inc.
All rights reserved.
    Library of Congress Card Catalog Number: 86-45342.
    International Standard Book Number: 0-89453-597-8.
Cover design by Brother Placid, OSB. Printed in the United States
of America.

Table of Contents

Editor's Preface

Up to quite recently mystics were either misunderstood or simply not understood. But now we are coming to see that, in T.S. Eliot's words, the way of the mystics is "our only hope, or else despair." As the darkness deepens, and the lights go out, those ancient lights begin to appear and to show us the way forward. They are not only lights to guide us, but are each a human countenance in which we can recognise something of ourselves – each is a portrait for self-recognition.

Unfortunately, the great Christian mystics have been generally presented as models of perfection or monuments of orthodoxy – sometimes, too, as inhumanly joyless and ascetical. Yet they were, above all else, men and women of feeling, always vulnerable, at times perhaps insecure and uncertain of the way ahead. For all that, they all shine with a special divine likeness and a special human radiance.

Each of the following portraits tries to present a true likeness of its subject, a likeness that comes alive especially in the ordinary and the everyday. In each case the author has been asked to enliven scholarship with personal warmth, and to temper enthusiasm with accurate scholarship. Each portrait hopes to be in its own way a work of art, something carefully and lovingly fashioned out of genuine material.

The main focus nevertheless is on the way in which each mystic mediates the Christian Gospel, and so gives us a deeper, richer, clearer vision of the Christian mystery. This kind of exposition demands the reader's full and prayerful attention. Each book is the story of a pilgrimage, for the mystic, the writer and the reader.

Noel O'Donoghue

Foreword

This little book is at once a study of a fifth-century text and a portrait of the writer of this text, who names himself as Patricius, the son of one Calpornius, a Christian deacon and a Roman *decurio* or alderman. The text is in Latin of a kind called Vulgar or Colloquial Latin, the spoken language of Romanised Gaul and Romanised Britain at that time. It seems more likely that Patrick came from Britain than from Gaul, probably from southwest Scotland, though the claims of England and Wales cannot be easily dismissed. One thing is certain: Patrick was *not* an Irishman.

Patrick was a Celt and belonged to that Celtic people which the Romans named the *Britanii*. He was also a Roman citizen and, like St. Paul before him, made use of the advantages this gave him to forward his work as a Christian missioner. He came to love the Irish and even at times to identify with them, yet it is clear that he never ceased to feel a sense of exile and the need to be accepted by his own people.

The *Confession* is a letter in defence of his life-work, and it was preceded by a shorter letter written to the followers of a local British leader named Coroticus, who had taken prisoner many of Patrick's converts and proposed to sell them into slavery, as Patrick himself had been sold as a boy of sixteen. In the present book I am mainly concerned with the *Confession* but will refer now and then to this other letter.

The life and mission of St. Patrick is an area of much scholarly controversy; indeed there is a dispute as to whether there were one, two or three Patricks. The world of Patrician scholarship is a fascinating one, but I have tried to keep clear of it. I am concerned with a text and with the author of that text. The text is well authenticated, and the portrait that emerges from the text is at once human and vulnerable, and yet endowed with spiritual power and that mystical fire and illumination that can best be seen as descending directly from the Father of lights.

The *Confession* may appear at first reading an unremarkable document, indeed as little more than the somewhat rambling reminiscences of a man of action who writes only with difficulty and by leaning heavily on scriptural quotations and references. It is only gradually that the reader begins to glimpse, to hear and to feel, the mighty spiritual force that is always pushing through the text. The main purpose of the present book is to express something of this by letting the text speak for itself: *for* itself and *to* us here and now, as we seek to know ourselves and to know what mysterious source from which we came and to which we seek to return.

The Select Bibliography provides indications of how to attain access to the original Latin text and to some of the best contemporary translations. I have worked directly on this Latin text as edited by Hanson after Bieler. A readable nineteenth century translation is given in an appendix as an accompaniment of the present exposition and interpretation. A second appendix reprints a poem on St. Patrick written some fifty years ago by Eugene Mullen, an Irish teacher who later became a Carmelite priest. It is very much in the oracular style of the epoch of Chesterton and Belloc —indeed it seems that Belloc praised the poem highly — and it embodies some of the confusions and legends that have surrounded St. Patrick over the centuries. But it deals nobly with the mystical heights and depths of the writer of the *Confession*, and it has also provided the present book with its title.

Isle of Iona.

1

Patrick the Dreamer

There were two sources of light in the world of Patrick, son of Calpornius, the author of the two letters named the *Confession* and the *Letter to Coroticus*: Holy Scripture and his own dreams.

Here I want to look at his dreams.

The *Confession* is a short document, about the length of an article for a theological magazine, yet it contains seven distinct dream narratives, and it is quite clear that each is seen as vitally important by Patrick himself. They are various and striking, and so vividly told that they, more than the recital of events, give liveliness and freshness to the narrative.

The first dream (or pair of dreams) comes in the context of his deep prayer-experiences during the latter part of his six-year captivity in Ireland. "My spirit was all on fire, and there on a certain night in my sleep I heard a voice saying to me: *it is well for you to fast for you are soon to go back to your own country.*" Shortly after this the words came to him (whether in his sleep or awake, he does not say): *your ship is ready.* And so he sets out on the long and hazardous journey back to his own country.

Now the first and most striking characteristic of this first recorded dream in Patrick's story is that it has its centre in a clear statement which needs little or no interpretation. Most of Patrick's dreams are of this kind. They are clear and remarkably concise messages. Neither Freud nor Jung is of any relevance here, at least as regards interpretation. The context of the dream is clear enough, as is also the fact that it is something heard rather than seen, as in fact are most of Patrick's similar experiences. What is not so clear is the manner of the hearing: did he awaken to recall having heard these words in a dream, or did he awaken out of sleep to hear these words? On the two occasions when there is a question of something seen, Patrick has a Scripture phrase at hand (from the Book of Daniel and elsewhere) and he is obviously very happy to use it: *visio* or *visus noctis*, a vision of the night. There is no parallel phrase for things heard, but he sometimes uses the word *responsum*, which in fact occurs six times in the course of the *Confession*, usually in the form *responsum divinum*, a divine response. However in the case of this first very important message the word *responsum* is not used, and there is probably a distinction to be made between locutions which come as an answer or response to prayer and the sudden, unexpected and totally receptive experience described in this first dream. This division between the divine monologue, or better the other-worldly monologue, and the divine partnership in the dialogue of prayer runs all through Patrick's account of his visionary experiences.

This first dream (17) is a promise of liberation and it was followed by a *responsum* which simply said: "Look, your ship is ready." But Patrick goes on to say that the ship was not near but in fact two hundred miles away. How did he know this? And how did he know where exactly it was? One has to assume, I think, a kind of continuity of guidance which would have been the accompaniment of continuous prayer. In other words, Patrick's dreams and responses must be seen as part of a life-style which had grown out of his discovery of prayer as an exile and a slave. There is here a kind of unity of sleeping and waking in a special life-style, of a kind that has not been much understood or examined. There must be a sense in which the man or woman of prayer and religious devotion and concern has a different "surround" in the mysterious world of sleep from that of the secular-minded or selfish or destructive person.

As we go on and examine Patrick's further dream-experiences a strange and terrifying world begins to open up. At least this is the ambience of the second dream recorded in the *Confession*. It comes at the end of an episode in which Patrick has prayed for food for his starving companions and has refused to offer some of it to the local deity. The experience has in its onset a nightmare quality; indeed what is described is the archetypal nightmare of oppression, suffocation and annihilating power. "It was as if a great rock fell on top of me, so that I could not move any part of my body" (20).

This experience happened many years before the *Confession* was written, when he was a young man in his early twenties, while the writer of the *Confession* sees himself as an old man: "this is my confession before I die" (62). Yet after forty years or more the experience is still vivid, still terrifying: "I shall remember it as long as I am in this body," he tells us, using, as was his wont, a scripture phrase (2 Peter 1.13). He has no doubt but that this annihilating power is Satan (did he have St. Paul's "angel of Satan" in mind?) and comes to him as a temptation or test. For Patrick, as for the writers of the New Testament, as also for Christian consciousness up to Patrick's time and long after, indeed until comparatively modern times, Satan was seen as a mighty annihilating or destroying force whose naked presence was utterly terrifying to the human spirit. This contact brought a kind of living annihilation that was named the *peirasmos* or test; by comparison with this all other human ills including poverty, imprisonment, death and even torture, however terrible and fearful, were challenges to faith and trust in God. But the "test" brought the total undoing of lived annihilation — the total absence of God and all the messengers of goodness and mercy. There is here, nevertheless, a battle that has to be faced and faced most inescapably along the higher reaches of the upward journey. Yet the prayer of Jesus takes full account of this as we ask the Father not to lead us too far along this way: lead us not into (the depths of) temptation.

We must be careful not to confuse this unforgettable Satan-experience with the very forgettable, though immediately terrifying, nightmares which most people experience now and then, especially in youth, and as a result of some passing indisposition. Patrick would have had his nightmares and bad dreams like everybody else, and he knew well that this Satan-experience was of a totally different kind, that it was an encounter with a very positive and a very personal as well as an immensely powerful enemy.

We are at a kind of crossroads here in our reading of the *Confession*. Up to quite recently a certain kind of "logical analysis" joined hands with psychological reductionism to dismiss all such "relations" as illusory or superstitious. This approach is already going out of fashion as it is becoming clear that so-called scientific explanation is firmly grounded not in certainty but in uncertainty, and that there are more and more facts that cannot be dealt with in terms of physical measurement. We are being forced to question the paradigm or set of common assumptions on which science and the scientific approach has been based.[1] From another direction there has been a movement towards allowing a text such as the *Confession* to meet the reader according to his or her pre-understanding. This is sometimes called Receptionism and in its extreme form it loosens the text completely from its anchorage in the past and sees it as a language-event which has entered into the stream of human self-understanding. It seems to me that this represents a healthy challenge to the kind of historicism that claims that the minds and meanings of our far-off ancestors are closed off from us, allowing us

---

[1]The classical work here is Thomas Kuhn's *The Structure of Scientific Revolutions* 2nd edition, enlarged, Chicago and London: University of Chicago Press, 1970. More recently, authors such as F. Capra (*The Tao of Physics*, 1975) and Paul Davies (*God and the New Physics*, 1983) have set out to illustrate the emergence of new horizons in physical science. From another standpoint Stanley Rosen's *The Limits of Analysis* (1980) and, at a more popular level, Jacob Needleman's *The Heart of Philosophy* (1984) question the philosophical basis of the kind of empiricism and "analysis" that would deny "other regions" the status of reality, or of possible reality.

instead to open our ears to what they have said and to give it contemporary life in our midst.[2] Once we have freed Patrick's text from our own projections and prejudices and allowed it to speak to our deepest centre of experience and understanding, we are in a position to let it resonate in us, to let it happen to us. It is only after we have listened that we can rightly question it as to its ultimate reference and value.

For Patrick, then, this second dream-experience is an encounter with Satan. It is, as it comes in the text, connected with his refusal to have anything to do with the earth-god of his Irish companions. This refusal seems almost ungracious since all that was asked of him was to accord a kind of minimum recognition of the earth-god's role in providing the meat and honey which rescued them from famine. Of course we are not sure of the name or place of the god or gods which he refused to acknowledge. All he tells us is that they found some wood-honey (*mel silvestre*, usually translated as "wild honey") and offered him some, saying "this is immolated," and that he refused it. It may well be that the honey was being offered to the sun-god, and that we have here Patrick's first missionary act as a Christian, an act at once of affirmation of the Christian deity (*Dominus Deus meus*, "my own Lord and God" Patrick names him in a phrase that links his Confession with that of St. Augustine) and negation of the ancient Celtic and pre-Celtic sun-god (honoured in ancient times in certain parts of Ireland including one at Drumlusk near Kenmare, Co Kerry near to the mountains sacred to Anu or Dana, the two Paps of Dana, *Dhā Kee^k Anainn*).

It was "that same night" that Patrick had his never-to-be-forgotten Satan experience. If his work as a Christian missionary begins here then this is also a threshold or boundary experience, having about it some of the drama expressed so powerfully by John Milton in his *Ode on the Morning of*

[2]See *Truth and Method* by H. G. Gadamer (Sheed and Ward, 2nd English Edition, 1975); R. C. Holub, *Reception Theory: A Critical Introduction* London and New York: (Methuen, 1984).

Christ's Nativity, which is filled with half-regretful visions of the departure of the ancient gods to make room for the new and final manifestation of the divine power and presence. Milton is too great a poet not to pay honour, however paradoxically, to the power and glory of these gods: indeed the whole theme of the poem is not so much that light has shone into the darkness as that the greater light has superseded the lesser. It is only gradually and painfully that we are in recent times giving some theological recognition to an insight that the poetic imagination could not at any time escape, the insight that there is a real continuity between the old and the new, between paganism and Christianity. Later I shall try to look at the way this insight is inscribed in the folklore of Celtic Christianity. Here we are concerned with listening to that strange and powerful and finally mysterious account in which Patrick relates his unforgettable experience of the Adversary.

It is when we come to the second part of the account that we are face to face in a most mysterious and disconcerting way with the meeting or clash of the old and the new, a mysteriousness that is greatly increased if we assume that Patrick's companions were worshippers of the sun. For having described the paralysing experience of the mighty rock (that was Satan or an emissary of Satan), Patrick continues: "How did it come to me, ignorant in spirit as I was, to call on Elias? So it came about that I saw the sun rise in heaven and while I called out "Elias, Elias" with all my strength behold the splendour of the sun fell upon me and at once all heaviness left me, and I believe that Christ the Lord came to release me" (20).

Patrick is an exceedingly plain writer and does not use rhetorical devices, so we can take it that the question he raises here is quite real for him and also quite unanswerable for him. But the question is not: why should I call on Elias? but: how did I come to call on Elias *then*? How did I, *ignorant as I was*, come to call on Elias? The implication seems fairly clear: the older and wiser Patrick who is writing the *Confession* sees it as right and reasonable to call on Elias. He has come to see the place of Elias as the herald of Christ, the one who opens the pathway along which Christ comes. He would also have in mind the statement in James 5.17 that Elias was a man like

ourselves yet all-powerful in his prayer. All this and more
would have come later, for the Patrick of the captivity would
not have had a copy of the Bible at hand and would have had
to depend on his half-remembered boyhood lessons in Christian doctrine.

But there is something else in this passage. There is the
connection between Elias or Helias and *Helios*, the Greek for
"sun." According to Hanson, Patrick's contemporaries made
this connection, and this seems to be assumed in this passage:
Patrick calls out *Helias, Helias* and then the sun rises. The
connection between Christ and the sun is made explicitly
towards the end of the *Confession* (59, 60). Christ is the "true
Sun who will never perish." We must be careful here. It is easy
to see the sun as a symbol of Christ, to turn paganism into a
useful source of Christian metaphor. But we must ask ourselves whether this is *all* that Patrick means in his account of
his release from Satan. In its whole perceptual structure what
is in question here is a sun-experience, an experience of an
illuminative source. It is not an experience of a human face or
a human figure any more than the Satan-experience is personal in the way, for example, the Satan-experience of Julian
of Norwich is personal. On the other hand, the experience is
not simply a physical sunrise experience though it is expressed
in terms of such an experience. Of course it can be said, as
indeed Hanson says, that it is all a dream experience, yet even
if it is all bracketed by sleep and only remembered on awakening we have to ask ourselves what this "sun" connoted for the
man who wrote the *Confession*. It seems to me that one is
pushed towards postulating some kind of inner world
(etheric? astral? imaginal? . . . .) of which the ordinary visible -
physical is but a manifestation.[3]

---

[3]One result of the development mentioned in Note 1 (above) is the putting in
question of the simple two-tier world of matter and spirit which is the legacy of
Descartes. We are beginning to envisage the possibility of a plurality of intermediary
worlds and so recover again, painfully, a sense of the perceptual world in which not
only our present text was composed but also the Old and New Testaments as well as
almost all the world's sacred texts. This new consciousness is perhaps best illustrated
by the emergence over the past few years of magazines such as *Temenos* (Watkins,
London, and the Lindisfarne Press, West Stockbridge, Mass., U.S.A.), *Mystics*

But is this encounter with Satan really a dream in the sense that only the memory of it remains on awakening? Or is it rather an awakening into that strange world that lies around the doorway of sleep, a place of transfigured or terrifying reality? Who has not felt the power and presence of that world? Who has not encountered some entity at the doorway of sleep or the threshold of awakening and felt its challenging power as if of a messenger not from the world of sleep but from a world of higher or lower awakening? The world of the everyday is familiar and in various degrees manageable. It is this third world, the world that lies around the threshold, that for some people (perhaps for everybody at some time?) is the place of terrors known, half-known and unknown (though surmised and feared most of all). It is easy to push this world quickly aside on awakening, but how can we escape it as we face the doorway of sleep? Fortunately most people most of the time pass through this threshold quickly, unconsciously even. But for some there is the constant danger of lingering on the threshold, for others some kind of broken fall in sleep which opens up this uncanny world. For the mystic this is a place of very deep and special prayer, a sharing in Gethsemane, or more rarely, a place of vision and transfigured reality. Apart from that nobody has discovered a way of dealing with this vestibule world.[4]

It seems to me that Patrick's unforgettable contact with Satan was an awakening threshold experience. He awakened to this oppression and paralysis, yet this awakening was not at all an opening to the everyday and its content of familiar things and people, but to a full consciousness of an annihilating power. The paralysis of which Patrick speaks is most of all terrifying in that it effectively closes off the familiar and everyday, what Thomas Gray calls "the warm precincts of this

Quarterly (Iowa, USA) and *Studies in Mystical Literature* (Taiwan). In all these highly responsible and academically reputable productions the place of "inner" or "other" worlds is taken seriously. From this perspective Patrick's experiences of the sun cannot be fully understood in terms of the physical sun understood literally or metaphorically.

[4]One helpful book is *Nightmare* by Sandra Shulman (London, 1979).

cheerful day." It is a place of total alienation, eternal loneliness. It is the place of the absence of the Father, the place of the absence of the Mother, of the absence of all companionship. Eros is dead; all trace of "the right human face" has disappeared. In this experience consciousness is awakened to its highest lucidity, being, as it were, held in an endless moment of felt annihilation. Here a man or woman is buried alive, alone and lost for ever. "It was as if a mighty rock fell on top of me." This is the unforgettable interminable moment. This is the experience of living death described by Gerard Manley Hopkins in his "terrible sonnets" witten towards the end of his life. Patrick is given release from this terror, yet he knows that this is pure gift and that there are no resources within himself that could call forth this gift. It is here above all that for him the spirit of man makes contact with the Holy Spirit of God, not as possession but as hope. I shall return to this in connection with the Holy Spirit. Just now I want to go forward into the sunlight which shone upon Patrick and released him from a captivity more painful than any human master could devise. He returns to his own people and *patria* (17) a free man who would nevertheless carry all his life the scars of captivity.

Patrick's description of his return home is full of warmth and a sense of belonging. Clearly he is important to his family and friends, and they use all their powers of persuasion to try to prevail on him to remain. Ireland, "the land at the world's end" (38), must have seemed an alien and savage world to these Romano-Britons, and it is clear that Patrick himself was of this mind and indeed never quite relinquished a certain racial prejudice. Nevertheless he decided to return to Ireland, and he made this decision because of a dream (23). It was a remarkably clear and vivid dream, yet for all that rather strange. In the dream Patrick saw a man coming towards him, "as if from Ireland," and the man's name was Victoricus. This man brought with him "innumerable letters," and gave one of them to Patrick. Patrick saw that this letter was entitled "The Voice of the Irish", and as he read these words he heard voices, the voices of people living "near the wood of Foclut by the western sea." These voices called out to him together: "We

beg you holy youth to come and walk again amongst us."
Patrick was so pierced by this cry that he could not read any
further, and he immediately awoke.

There has been much discussion among Patrician scholars
as to the location of "the wood of Foclut" (*silva Focluti*) and
also as to the authenticity of "holy youth" (*sancte puer*), but
neither of these matters affect the substance or significance of
the dream, and it is with this I am concerned here. The
narrative is simple and the structure is clear. There is first
vision, then hearing, and finally feeling. It is this latter especially that is underlined: "I was deeply pierced in my heart"
(*valde compunctus sum corde*). Obviously this links up with
the various heart-piercings of the Old and New Testament:
Hanson refers us to Acts 2.37 where the Jews and strangers
who heard Peter's Pentecost speech were "cut to the heart"
and asked to be baptized; this passage in turn echoes other
text in the Old and New Testament. All this the writer of the
Confession would have known; here as elsewhere he is placing
his own experience in a scriptural context. In the context of
Acts, however, the piercing or *compunctio* is the effect of the
voice of God as mediated by his prophet or apostle; in
Patrick's case it is "the voice of the Irish" that has this effect. If
those "by the wood of Foclut" were sitting in pagan darkness
one would have expected a response of pity and compassion,
and Scripture is full of such words. It is hard to escape the
impression that Patrick had already made some soul-friends
in Ireland, who may indeed have already, either through
Patrick himself or otherwise, accepted Christianity. We know
that there was a pre-Patrician Christianity, and it is significant
that the voices in the dream do not ask for preaching or
baptism but only that Patrick as one specially endowed
(*sancte puer*) should come back and share their lives: come
and walk once more (*adhuc*) with them. Patrick was being
asked to return to a situation of friendship, receptivity and
mutual concern about holiness of life. If this is the case then
the traditional reading of the *Confession* as an account of a
kind of "invasion" of Christianity into a pagan world has to be
revised.

There are many parallels between St. Patrick and St. Paul,

not least the fact that both were led into a large missionary undertaking by a dream. If it is remarkable that Christianity, at least in its full power and presence, came to Ireland by way of a dream, it is no less remarkable that it was in this way also that Christianity came to Europe. The story is told in the sixteenth chapter of the Acts of the Apostles, and it acts as a kind of hinge holding together the third person narrative of the first fifteen chapters and the first person narrative of the remaining chapters. This is how St. Luke tells the story: "In the course of the night a vision was seen by Paul. A man of Macedonia stood before him and called to him saying: *Come over to Macedonia and help us.* When he had seen this vision we began at once to plan our course for Macedonia, having decided that God had summoned us to preach the Gospel there." Patrick, who was very much a man of one book, would have known this story well, and it is possible that it provided the structure for his own dream. Certainly it would have provided a warrant for thinking that God works in this way, though of course he could find ample grounds both in the Old and New Testaments for supposing that God could reveal his purposes in dreams and visions.

Patrick's missionary dream is followed immediately — at least as he tells his story — by two further dreams which serve to provide deep inner foundations for his future work. I shall deal with these in the next chapter, for they must be seen in the context of Patrick's relationship to the Holy Spirit. They involve a kind of "speaking in tongues," or more exactly a kind of "inner speaking," and I shall try to understand them in the wider context of Patrick's spirit-experiences. The final dream narrative has to do with what may be called his Judas-experience, and this also needs to be looked at in the context of Patrick's sensitive and vulnerable personality.

But before leaving the direct treatment of Patrick's dream experiences, it is necessary to face the theological question of the place of dreams in the Christian understanding of God's activity and man's response and responsibility.

Traditionally — at least in recent times — the topic of dreams receives hardly a reference in Christian theology, Catholic or Protestant. There is very little about it in the

Pre-Vatican II Catholic manuals such as Noldin and Prümmer, and what is there is largely negative, being mainly concerned with dreams as a form of divination and therefore reprehensible. However, when we go back to St. Thomas Aquinas and take in also his sixteenth century commentaries, we find a much more positive treatment of dreams, a treatment that in fact gives full warrant to Patrick's reliance on dreams. For not only does Thomas deal negatively with dreams as a form of divination, but he also deals positively with dreams when he comes to deal with the charism of prophecy. Briefly he teaches that dreams may be a means by which God communicates to people by way of enlightenment or practical direction. This communication as it comes from its divine source is appropriated to the Holy Spirit but more proximately comes through the ministry of angels as God's ministers. However, this angelic ministry makes use of human imagination and is closely linked with the free play of images in sleep. In sleep we are sensitive not only to angelic or demonic manipulation but also to the impression of our own bodily moods from within, and also to the natural environment around us including the world of the heavenly bodies. Sleep, for Thomas, liberates the imagination, *virtus imaginativa*, for good and ill, for truth and falsehood, for clarity and confusion, though, of course, responsible decision belongs to the waking self.[5]

All in all, Thomas provides a remarkably positive account of the dream as a vehicle of knowledge. It is in sleep that the

[5]St. Thomas' negative approach to dreams (as a form of divination) is to be found in *Summa Theologiae* II a IIae Q95, art 6 under the general heading of *Divinatio*. It is this treatment that has led authors such as Morton Kelsey to see St. Thomas and Thomism as generally opposed to dreams as part of authentic religious experience (see Kelsey's *Dreams: A Way to Listen to God*, Paulist Press, 1978) p. 19. However, when he comes to deal with the subject of prophecy further on in the same book (QQ 171, 172) Thomas provided the very positive and balanced analysis which I have summarised. (See also *S. Theol.* I, Q 91 art. 3). There are many contemporary books on dreams and dreaming; among those I have consulted I found *Dream Work* by Jeremy Taylor especially challenging and comprehensive (Paulist Press, 1983). Among Christian theologians Kelsey has done good pioneering work on the theology of dreams, (see especially *Dreams: The Dark Speech of the Spirit*, Doubleday, 1968).

mind, released from its concern with the physical world clam-
oring for attention, is receptive of "the more subtle influences
of nature and in touch with higher spheres" (Q172.1 and 1).
The area of "the subtle influences of nature"includes the body
and psyche (i.e. the soul or *anima* as operating in and through
the body) and what came later to be called "the unconscious,"
but Thomas' account of dreams leaves room also not only for
the physical background and foreground of sleep but also for
the whole immense and mysterious world of angels and demons and whatever may be thought of as surrounding the
portals of sleep.

Thomas' doctrine may be traced back in its essentials to the
early scholastics such as Isidore of Seville and to the Patristic
period contemporary with Patrick's Confession, and of
course it has ample warrant in the Old and New Testament as
Thomas points out, as also in the philosophical tradition to
which Thomas belongs, both Platonic and Aristotelian. On
the other hand, it must be said that for Thomas and the
tradition which he represents the world of dreams is not seen
as part of normal human living but is allowed its say only in
the exceptional experience of "prophecy." So it is that this
world does not appear at all in Thomas' detailed and comprehensive account of the human person to which the second
part of the *Summa Theologiae* is largely devoted. It comes up
for positive discussion only in a kind of extended appendix to
this second part, which begins at question 171. Dreams are
seen as having a place within the charism of prophecy, which is
not a matter of common and universal human behavior, but
rather of gifts which are given for the purpose of building up
the Christian community.

So it is that though Thomas and the tradition which he so
brilliantly presents allows ample place for Patrick's world of
dreams, there is a profound difference of atmosphere. Dreams
are felt differently by Patrick and Thomas: for Patrick they
are deeply interwoven with Christian experience; for Thomas
they are optional and peripheral. The Aristotelian theologian
makes room for Patrick's dreams but is distinctly uncomfort-
able with Patrick the dreamer.

2

The Experience of God the Father

Perhaps the most famous legend connected with Patrick is that of the explanation of the Trinity or Triunity by way of the shamrock. The story is that the Irish disciples of Patrick had difficulty with the understanding of a God who is at one and the same time one and three. So Patrick stooped down and picked up a shamrock and showed how it was at once three and one. Apparently the Irish were satisfied with the explanation and have never wavered in their trinitarian orthodoxy from that day to this.

This is, of course, pure legend. There is nothing about it in the *Confession* nor in the Coroticus Letter, nor does this kind of pedagogy fit in with the tone of Patrick's exposition, which is in the mode of witness rather than explanation. But a legend has its own kind of truth, and there is no doubt but that Patrick was a very earthed man. It seems that his enemies called him *Magunios*, the Pigman, and we know from the *Confession* that he was a herdsman. He was not a man of books but of everyday chores and concerns. He met the green fields and rainy skies of Ireland before he met its people. There is a sense in which he felt his way into the Christian faith through long and painful contact with the elements. "My home was the woods and the mountain," he tells us, "and I would awaken before the light of day to pray even in times of snow and ice and rain"(16). This is the kind of prayer in which a man unites earth and heaven through what Hubert van Zeller calls "the springs of the Benedicite." It can be said that Patrick did indeed meet with the Triune God where the shamrock grows and blows in the green fields and quiet woodland and windswept hills of Ireland. Indeed this wrestling with the elements and with his change of status from that of the son of a well-regarded Roman family to that of the slave of a barbarian master was but the outer expression of an inner wrestling with that strange, terrible and all-absorbing being whom he "acknowledged and adored as one God in the sacred invocation of the Trinity" (4).

Patrick received his early and later Christian formation at a time when the Trinitarian formulation had been fixed, and he received it without question. He was not a speculative theologian, and from this point of view his writings belong to the history of belief rather than the history of theology. Yet by way of ascetical and visionary experience he felt his way to the very centre of Christian theology, especially and pre-eminently the Christian theology of the Trinity. Briefly it can be said that he met each of the Three Divine Persons personally, so that the *Confession* is at one level the story of this encounter.

In the first place his fall out of human fathering into fatherless slavery became a living encounter with the Fatherhood of God. The passage at the beginning of the *Confession* in which he recalls this experience after many years is full of tenderness and pathos, and shows how the shape of his new experience and his new consciousness became the profile of a filial countenance reflecting the Father's countenance, where sternness dissolves into compassion, and compassion dissolves into love. Indeed Patrick sees his captivity as an expression of the Father's wrath: "Behold I will fill this people with wormwood and give them poisonous water to drink. I will scatter them among the nations whom neither they nor their fathers have known; and I will send the sword after them until I have consumed them" (Jer. 9.15-16). Having quoted from this passage Patrick immediately brings it into relationship with a passage from the Acts of the Apostles which gives an entirely positive and hopeful context to this devastating wrath. What Patrick writes is: *God scattered us among the nations* (Jer. 9.15) *even to the ends of the earth* (Acts 13.47). The whole passage in Acts reads: "I have set you to be a light for the Gentiles, that you may bring salvation to the ends of the earth." The Father's chastising power becomes the Father's saving purpose, and Patrick finds his own humility and elevation in the midst of it. The phrase he uses to express his situation is an original one, and it has the sharpness and beauty of a personal signature: *parvitas mea*, "my littleness." From the beginning to the end of the *Confession* this is Patrick's self-conscious and self-identifying image. It becomes manifest first by his fall into slavery, but this outer condition is later replaced by an equally humiliating inner condition: his lack of education. His way, like the way of Thérèse of Lisieux 1500 years later, is a way of littleness that opens up in total trust to the Father's love.

Patrick's first step into the world of the invocation of the Trinity is an existential opening to the Father as stern judge and compassionate lover, existential in the sense that it expresses his deepest desire and concern, his mind's horizon and the light by which he journeys on. "Man is strangest of all strange beings," said Sophocles, "for he is always a wayfarer, always on a journey." Patrick's journey is discovered in his discovery of the Father's love and purposes: this is the true journey of every Christian missioner, of which the voyages over sea and land are but the outward expression.

It is, I think, important from the point of view of Patrick's trinitarian experience to see that he passes in the first paragraph of the *Confession* from the Godhead to the personal Father who is the first or source Person of the Trinity, and who is understood in deep personal relationship to Patrick himself. Here he employs quite unconsciously a method at once invocational and descriptive which sees the Father in relation to his own childhood and boyhood, not as a stage that is superseded but as a deep filial relationship that remains always valid and full of wonder and gratitude. In fact the way back to childhood (or boyhood) is at the same time the way forward to that spiritual or mystical childhood which Christ puts at the very heart of his moral teaching, just as the filial relationship with the Father is at the heart of his revelation of the Godhead.

All this is expressed with clarity and force in the second and third paragraphs of our text. It is a passage full of haunting tenderness, and it falls strangely on our twentieth century ears, for ours is the time of the rejection of that filial love that flows back to the human source of our being, and so we do not have any real and deeply felt access to God the Father. We live in the time of the death of the father and the time of the death of God: the time of the drying up of the source. All this happens within human consciousness. Human fatherhood goes on, however brokenly; the divine source does not fail or diminish, nor does it lose its morning freshness nor the delight of creative love. It is that "beauty ever ancient and ever new" which Augustine discovered in his more liberated and liberating moments, before that same beauty and glory became frozen in the paralysis of predestination.

It is indeed right to recall at this point that other *Confession* written within the same century as that of Patrick, that of Augustine of Hippo, whose light and whose shadow lies across Western Christendom. Later I shall try to look at this comparison (and contrast) in some specific ways. Here I want to remark on the striking identity of tone that binds the two together in this matter of the filial love of the all-fathering God. In both cases the Godhead, the one divine essence or nature, tends to take on the personal countenance of the Father, and this is especially evident in the phrase *Dominus Deus Meus*, "the Lord my God," used freely by both Patrick and Augustine. Yet we must be careful in reading these glowing texts not to allow the personal countenance of the Father to become depersonalized and to disappear into the mysterious abyss of the Deity. Patrick believes indeed in the Godhead of the Triune God, that is, *One* in Three, but it is the Father that he has met, and it is the Father's countenance that meets him in his prayers. Indeed the whole of the *Confession* is a prayer of thanksgiving to the Father who came to him and consoled him in his captivity "as a (human) father consoles his child" (2).

Patrick's condition is the slave-condition, and his tender and totally dependent relationship with the Father is by no means peripheral to Christian or religious experience. It was to become the situation of his spiritual heirs for centuries in the country of his own slave-experience and missionary experience: only those who are totally ignorant of Irish history can question this. Indeed the voice of the *Confession* becomes the "voice of the Irish" as calamity follows calamity for three hundred years, culminating in the Great Famine of the mid-nineteenth century. The link with the Christian slave who tended sheep and pigs in all weathers has been forged again and again in the depths of Irish self-apprehension, so that the triumphalism of St. Patrick's Day celebrations has, for all its exaggerations, its holy ground in authentic experience. It expresses a repeatable possibility, at both the personal and national level, of living again the consoling and liberating love of the One that Patrick encountered when he lay "like a stone deep in the mire" (12). The same existential situation is described in James H. Cone's article "The Meaning of God in the Negro Spirituals."[6] Cone argues that there is always in the religious expression of the slave-situation a sense of the Father as not only the Consoler but the Liberator as well. The reconciliation of acceptance with protest (even unto blood) is a delicate matter, and it is the very heart-beat of Irish history even up to the present day. It is already there in that other and lesser writing of Patrick, the *Letter to the Soldiers of Coroticus*. In this letter the voice of pain passes over not only into acceptance and the assurance of divine help and retribution but also into a cry of human protest directed to human ears.

The cry of the slave that rises upwards to God the Father is always and everywhere a cry for liberation. Yet it is also, strangely, a cry of fellowship and belonging, and this is something of a depth and intimacy immeasurable in its possibilities and inconceivable in its inner logic. Part of this possibility is

[6]In *God as Father?* (Edinburgh: T and T Clark, New York: Seabury Press, 1981).

indeed measurable, inasmuch as the deeper the abjection the more intimate the cry and the more naked the need. So, too, the first steps of this logic may be conceived of clearly: since I do not own myself (which is the essence of slavery) I must seek to be owned in my totality by the God of my life. But it is beyond this possibility, beyond these considerations, that the prayer of the slave begins, so that he sings in his chains. Thus it is that the greatest song of the love of man for God that Western Christendom has heard came forth from a narrow prison-cell in Toledo: the *Spiritual Canticle* of St. John of the Cross.

Patrick's slave-song expressed itself in the rhythms of day and night and the changes of season and weather. "A hundred times in the day and almost as often in the night I gave myself to prayer," he recalls, wondering in his old age at the force and fervour of that continuous exchange with his heavenly lover, for this melody belongs to the past, to the slave-time of his journey. "There was no sloth in me then such as I find in myelf now for at that time there was fire in my heart" (16).

Simone Weil remarks that we do not see the face of God because we look upwards when we should look downwards — to the face of the crucified and totally humiliated Christ.[7] This is the true reflection of the Father's countenance in the depths of a world ruled by hypocrisy and cruelty. The face of the slave-boy at prayer "in snow and ice and rain before the first light of day" (16) reflects the face of the Father; the heart of the slave-boy all aglow in lonely places "in the woods and on the mountain" is the heart of the Father reaching down to a people who sit in darkness and long for light. At this point all the earthly metaphors and analogies disappear into a human face and a human heart that is at once child and man, at once yin and yang, ever ancient and ever new. As we look at that radiant face of the slave-boy at prayer, at the face, tear-stained and luminous, dimly apparent against the brightening east — as we share this event we begin to realise how

---

[7]I cannot find the exact reference, but the theme of the power of suffering is explored in *Gateway to God* (Collins, 1974) pp. 87ff.

totally mistaken, indeed how vulgar and trivial, is all talk of God the Father as authoritarian and patriarchal, how impertinent it is to speak of *Him* or *Her*. For we have here in the whole radiant being of the slave-boy revealed in this prayer a glimspe of the Source whose name is Love. Whether deep in the woods or high in the hills we are in a place where all controversy is transcended. Far away in the east and in the south men are locked in controversy about the Three-in-One and the Man who is God. Patrick, a slave among the pagans, is discovering the Trinity by a living encounter with each of the Eternal Persons, beginning with the Father who meets him in lonely places and becomes his daily and nightly companion. In all this he is following very closely in the footsteps of Jesus of Nazareth, who would also arise before dawn to pray in lonely places (Mark 1.35) and used to spend whole nights in the communion of prayer with that Father-God whom the world did not know (Luke 5.16; 6.12; John 17.25).

3

The Discovery of Jesus Christ

I have argued that Patrick found the Face of God the Father (or of the Father-God) in his self-understanding as a slave, alone, bereft of human father and *patria*, "lying like a stone in the mire." The face of the Father began to delineate itself as the reverse image of the face of the slave, as in the story of the Prodigal Son, where the Father's image only reveals itself when the young man finally saw his own face by realising his servant-condition. Patrick returns again and again to this experience either directly (27) or indirectly by an almost obsessive realisation of the continuing result of this experience which shows itself in his lack of learning and his rejection by his peers.

Now this road that leads to the Father, this reverse image of the face of the Father, becomes at a certain point a road leading to the discovery of the Son in the face of Jesus Christ, God and man. We must be careful here lest in apprehending what may be called the Christological formula we miss the immediacy of the experience.

But first let us look at the formula in itself. It has been called Patrick's Rule of Faith, and Dr. Hanson has linked it with the catechetical practice of Patrick's day as represented by Victorinus of Pettau. But here I am principally concerned with the words written by Patrick, both in their own expressiveness and in the human personality which is their immediate source. In other words, since Patrick does not try in any way to call this part (or any part) of the *Confession* a Rule of Faith, I shall not treat it as such but see it simply as part of the narrative as it unfolds.[8]

Well, then: after the discovery of God the Father, at once as God and as Father, Patrick goes on, "For there is no other God, nor was there ever nor will there ever be except God the Father unbegotten and without beginning, from whom all things begin and who holds all things together as we affirm; and his Son Jesus Christ who was always with the Father, as we testify, being begotten of the Father before the beginning of time and before all beginning in a spiritual manner that is beyond all description; and through him were made all visible and invisible things; having become man and gained the victory over death he was received into the Heavens by the Father, who gave him all power over every name in heaven, on earth and in hell so that every tongue might confess that Jesus Christ is Lord and God; in whom we believe and look towards in the expectation of His coming in the near future as Judge of the living and, the dead who will render to each according to his deeds."

The central affirmation here is that Jesus Christ, *God and man*, is from eternity. How then can it be said that the same Jesus Christ became man at a certain moment in time? This difficulty is recognised in the words *spiritaliter* (in a spiritual manner) and *inenerrabiliter* (beyond all description). These are not so much explanatory terms as indications that we are being brought into a transintellectual zone. At least this is clearly the import of *inenarribiliter*; *spiritaliter* says a little more, and indeed gives a slant to the text which is theologically of the greatest interest. A century before the *Confession* was written the very orthodox (to us) Athanasius and the unorthodox (to us) Appollinaris held that the soul or spirit of

---

[8]See Hanson's note *In loco*, and the references he provides. Still relevant is J. E. L. Oulton's *The Credal Statements of St. Patrick* (London: Oxford U.P., 1940).

Jesus Christ was divine and uncreated.[9] This view was rejected at the Council of Chalcedon where it was affirmed that Jesus Christ had a full human nature including a human soul and (in a later clarification) a full human will. Patrick's use of the word *spiritaliter* seems to imply this.

Yet if we look at the text more closely we see that what is affirmed is not the eternal existence of a logos-soul that later enters a human body, but rather the eternal existence of the same human and divine being who was born in time at the incarnation. Not just the Second Person of the Trinity, not just the Son of God, but also Jesus Christ, the Son of Man, is from eternity.

Patrick does not mention the Virgin Mary, the historical and time-enclosed woman, and because of this omission the historical incarnation becomes loosened from its anchorage in history. It is indeed a historical fact, but it is as much a taking up of history into eternity as a coming down of etenity into history.

In Patrick's Christology the Incarnation is described in two words which are, so to speak, dropped in to the narrative: *hominem factum*. The implied reference to John 1.14 is clear, yet what Patrick read there was *verbum caro factum est*: the *Word* was made flesh. He is indeed very far from wishing to offer an alternative formula to express the mystery of the Incarnation, yet Patrick has excluded himself from the context of the Johannine formula by beginning with Jesus Christ rather than with the Eternal and pre-incarnate Logos who, dramatically, becomes flesh and dwells amongst us. What Patrick is affirming (as indeed Karl Barth has done in our time) is the pre-historical existence of the man named Jesus of Nazareth, the Anointed Saviour.[10]

The narrative as it continues maintains this "high" and "heavenly" note. Having become man Jesus Christ conquers death, is received into the heavens by the Father, given Lordship over Heaven, Earth and Hell, and will soon come back to

---

[9]"In the Alexandrian picture of Christ the bright light of the Logos swallows up any created light." A. Grillmeier, *Christ in the Christian Tradition* Vol 1, 2nd ed. (London: Membrays, 1975) p. 325.

[10]See A. T. Hanson, *The Image of the Invisible God* (S. C. M. Press, 1982).

Earth to pass judgment on the living and the dead. This is indeed Christ the Warrior and the Victor who takes every-thing in his stride "as a giant who runs his course." The Face of God has indeed become a human face, but a human face that is far off and inaccessible.

Or so it would seem until we realise that this face is shining on a boy who not only is a slave but a slave who has fallen into this condition and is therefore totally conscious of what it is and who he is within it. It is through this self-realization and this self-image that the image of the true and perfect sonship of Jesus Christ reveals itself. This other human face is the corrective and fulfilling image by which Patrick's experience is fully grasped and explored.

Patrick has discovered the existential meaning of slavery as a human possibility, or as providing the ground of a human possibility of reflecting the divine immensity as a quiet lake reflects the firmament. He had been brought into that very dark place where the light of the Beatitudes can be discovered through an inner spirit-vision. Blessed are the poor...the meek...those that mourn...the persecuted: *makarios*, the word we translate 'blessed', opens up the heavenly spaces and the Father's countenance reflected fully in the human form of Jesus Christ.

The Face of Christ is the Human Face of God but also the Divine Face of Man by which all men are judged, of him "who renders to each according to his deeds." There is no hint of predestination here, but a very straight affirmation of merit and reward, and it would seem that this remained a constant within the Celtic Church. Christ as Judge comes with no presuppositions or preferences but rather as total and terrify-ing justice and fairness. Yet we are not in the Greek world of absolute and abstract justice and necessity; the Judge has, after all, a human face.

With judgment goes power. Patrick's Christ is like the Spanish ikon of *El Cristo de Gran Poder*: a towering figure, impregnable, invulnerable, imposing his presence on the whole vast amphitheatre of creation. It was thus St. Paul saw him, and Patrick is ready to share this vision fully. It is a dangerous vision by which all too easily Satan can hide in the face of Christ; it is the self-image by which Christ Himself was tempted and after which the Adversary left him "for a while" (Luke 4:13). At any rate the face of Christ as it appears to Patrick in this general statement of his faith is touched with the cold and cruel light of absolute power. Obviously Patrick found the elements of this portrait in the New Testament; indeed it is set down in New Testament colours, but there is question here not of the elements of the portrait one by one, which are found in the New Testament in wide and balanced context, but of the isolation of these particular elements to form a brief composite portrait that can only be described as cold and forbidding.

But we must ask how far this portrait of Christ emerges from Patrick's own experience. Here it will help to distinguish three aspects of this experience: the experience of slavery, the experience of prayer and the experience of mission. We have seen that Patrick's experience of slavery, consciously experienced as such, opened the way to the vision of the Father and to the vision of Jesus Christ as the eternal Son of the Father. The Father was *with* him in this experience, and so was Jesus Christ the all-powerful Judge of the living and the dead. But Christ was with him in another way also, as a companion in slavery and abjection, as sharing the condition of *paupertas* which was given its evangelical mening by his presence. This condition of *paupertas* can scarcely be described in the word "poverty" with its implication of greyness and drabness. For the ancient Christian imagination *paupertas* is illuminated by the heavenly glow of the beatitudes, and is full of the hope and the excitement of going forth to preach the Gospel. From this point of view Patrick's slave-experience and missionary-experience are bound together: in both he is the poor man whose poverty Christ Himself shares and illuminates. Again from this point of view *paupertas* is to be preferred to riches (55), presumably not only for Patrick himself but also for his Christian converts. He could from his point of view have prayed for no better gift for Ireland then and now than this *paupertas.* The Christian world has largely lost this kind of Christian imagination in our time but we cannot understand Patrick apart from it. Nor can we understand how the various experiences which can be included under *paupertas* become communion with and companionship with Christ, Christ no longer the Lord and Judge but Christ as emptied, self-emptied but truly emptied, of all that human imagination (falsely for the most part) attributes to divinity. The fellowship of *paupertas* has a curious intimacy about it, for it enters into all the needs and happenings of bodily existence in a way that is possible for no other form of companionship. So it is that the great Christian paradox is realised, that it is in weakness and abjection that man enters most fully into the joy and glory of heavenly companionship.

Patrick chose the poor as Christ did, and in this choice he had the companionship of Christ. But he also, and more profoundly, chose *paupertas* as most certainly (*certissime*) more right for him than riches or sufficiency. Yet this *paupertas* involved a kind of hand-to-mouth sufficiency, so what Patrick really rejects is a *secure* sufficiency, and it is this state of insecurity, not only as regards what are called the necessaries of life but also as regards safety and liberty, that unites him with Christ in the hidden glory of *paupertas*. The full vision of this glory had to await the coming of Francis of Assissi, but it was in its essential notion present already in Patrick's time and outstandingly in Patrick himself. Unless we grasp its nature we cannot understand Patrick's Christology.[11]

Patrick's experience of *paupertas* is continuous with his experience of slavery. So, too, his prayer-experience of Christ binds together the two main parts of his life represented by his two experiences of Ireland. The time of his captivity, or first captivity, culminates in his Elias-experience which passes over into a Christ-experience: "The Spirit of Christ cried out for me" (20). Later, at the time when he is preparing to return to Ireland, he has a similar night-experience in the course of which many words are spoken which he does not understand, but they culminate in the statement very clearly apprehended

---

[11]No more than Francis (or Paul or Christ himself) is Patrick concerned with poverty and oppression in terms of social and political justice. This concern can never be far from Christian consciousness, but the spiritual and mystical dimension of poverty shines forth in its own grandeur and glory. See *St. Francis of Assisi* by Leonardo Boff (Tr. Dierckmeir, London, 1985).

(*peritissime*): "He who gave his life for you is he who speaks in you" (24). And so he wakes up full of joy.

Here, as in the Elias-experience, we seem to be in the vestibule world between sleeping and waking. At the end of the experience there is a joyful awakening (*expertus sum*) yet Patrick opens his brief account of the experience by saying that he does not know whether it happened in him or near him. "I do not know, God knows," he says, clearly linking the experience with that of St. Paul when he was "caught up in to the third heaven and heard things that cannot be told" (2 Cor 12.2-3 RSV). Patrick also heard things that could not be told, but these were also things he could not understand, or rather *words* he could not understand — words very clearly heard and, it would seem, clearly remembered.

There is implied here a remarkable continuity between sleeping and waking, between day-vision and night-vision. And this is a "Christed" continuity, a total presence of Christ in and near Patrick, indeed at one and the same time in him and near him. This Christ presence goes with him into sleep and becomes his awakening sun, his awakening joy . It is impossible to miss here the echoes of the prayer called "St. Patrick's Breastplate": *Christ within me, Christ before me,* etc. Scholars generally place this prayer a century or more after Patrick's time, yet a passage like this one shows how well the Breastplate expresses the intimacy and depth of Patrick's Christ-consciousness.

The words of his dream-hearing which alone he undertands are in part a quotation from the first letter of John (3.16). The full original statement runs: *by this we know love, that he laid down his life for us, and we ought to lay down our lives for the brethren* (RSV). There is here an echo of the Good Shepherd passage in the Fourth Gospel: The Good Shepherd lays down his life for his sheep (10.11); Jesus, who is the good shepherd, lays down his life that he may take it up again (10.14). It would seem indeed that Patrick is conscious of the reference to this passage rather than the one in 1 John; and that there is a kind of "rounding" here of Patrick's own experience as a shepherd and his future pastor-presence among the Irish, all finding its centre and meaning in the shepherd-presence of Christ in Patrick's life. In the dream-experience which precedes this shepherd-dream Patrick has heard the "voice of the Irish" calling him back. Here it is the voice of the Christ-shepherd he hears, the voice which the sheep recognise (Jn 10.4).

The life which the Good Shepherd lays down is not mere physical life, nor is the death he dies mere physical death. It is rather soul-life, *anima,* which is in question, a life whose yielding up involves the very terror of annihilation, that "temptation" which falls across Patrick's whole being like a great rock (20) and which he later recalls when he speaks of himself as a living sacrifice in the yielding up of his own soul to the same Christ who gave up his soul for Patrick (34). This final, absolutely terrifying, sacrificial union with Christ is the vital and vitalising centre of the *Confession.* We shall return to it again in analysing Patrick's relationship with the Holy Spirit.

Patrick's missionary experience is at its deepest level a realisation and exploration of his vital union with the poverty and sufferings of Christ. At this deep level the fears and hardships which are his daily companions (53) are not seen as the unfortunate and partly disabling companions of the kind of mission he has undertaken; rather are these companions chosen in themselves precisely because they were the companions of Jesus Christ himself. Patrick knows that the call to follow Christ, the cost of true discipleship, is not in the first instance a call to preach the Good News but in the first place a call to follow after Christ all the way to Calvary. This is an imitational Christology carried to its logical conclusion, at all times the burden and glory of the monastic tradition. This is indeed a heavy burden, and a man or woman might well seek ways of escaping it as its full weight comes to be felt. Over the centuries Christians have discovered a thousand ways of escape and evasion, ways of softening the "hard sayings" of Christ while claiming full discipleship. Patrick's understanding of Christ, in the depths of the spirit of sacrifice that was also a sacrifice of the whole spirit or soul (*anima*), allowed no compromise in this matter.

It can be argued that this sacrificial Christ-consciousness has been one of Patrick's most significant legacies to the Irish Church.   But perhaps it is something central to the Celtic religious consciousness, both for good and ill, as it generated either harshness and intransigence on the one hand, or warmth and generosity on the other. This will come up again under the heading of the mystical element in Patrick's spirituality.

Here we are concerned with the strength and depth of Patrick's link with Christ in the mode of imitation leading to union and in the mode of union leading to identity.

It is this intimate Christology that balances and humanises that otherwise one-sided understanding of the Divine Personhood of Jesus Christ as far-off and inaccessible, barely touching human clay and the procession of human history. The Christ that Patrick encounters in his slave-experience, in his prayer-experience, and in his missionary activity is infinitely near and totally vulnerable.

The two Christologies come together in the Resurrection-Christology of glory. It is precisely from the depths of poverty and abjection, precisely from the death on the Cross, that this glory shines.   In a powerful passage towards the end of the *Confession* Patrick affirms the unconditional nature of his own union with the sacrificial death of Christ — not only death in the shedding of his blood but the tearing apart and consumption of his flesh by wild beasts and the birds of the air — and his total confidence that he will rise with Christ in glory (59).   He will rise "in the radiance of the sun, that is, in the glory of Christ Jesus, our Saviour." There is a certain imaginative power in Patrick's use of sharp and shocking images of destruction and degradation to give larger space for the glory to radiate.   Here again the depth and the height are in correlation as reverse images of each other. Only the depth can show forth the height; the depth must meet the demand of the height for manifestation. This is, of course, a common theme in St. Paul, and it is usually understood morally as commending the humility of the self-emptying of Christ and calling the Christian to follow Him in humility and service. Yet it has, for St. Paul as even more clearly for St. John, a deeper level of meaning as affirming what may be called an ontological structure, that is to say, an inner mystery or secret of *being*. Being is not static but active; it goes forth and returns, it moves (as Hegel saw) towards its own negation in order to express its inner possibilities, in order to radiate, in order to become *glory*. In this sense glory is the home-coming of being, a celebration of return which necessitates a going-forth undertaken in freedom. So it is that Jesus connects his return to the Father with a new emergence of a glory already there from the beginning (Jn 17).

Patrick does not, of course, speak in these terms, yet I think this insight is within him, unformulated yet struggling for expression. He knows that there is a work of glorification, the emergence of ancient glory, in the total newness of the Resurrection, and he knows that his whole being has been taken over by this process. This is a supremely joyful consciousness, but it is also supremely terrifying because it involves the giving away not only of his whole bodily being but of his soul as well (59). It seems to me that he lived, at least in his later life, in the shadow of this terror. Yet he lived in hope and in the comfort of the Holy Spirit, as I shall now try to show.

4

The Fellowship of the Holy Spirit

The *Confession* of Patrick is animated from beginning to end by the Holy Spirit, who is named as the Spirit (11, 43, 46), the Spirit of God (33), the Spirit of the Living God (11), the Spirit of the Father (20). It is remarkable that the Spirit is named the *Holy* Spirit only in the Trinitarin formulations that come near the beginning (11) and towards the end (60) of the *Confession*, and at the end of *Coroticus*.

At first sight it seems that the Spirit enters the narrative with this first Trinitarian formulation (11) which structures what has been called Patrick's Rule of Faith. Yet if we read the text in this way we run the risk of enclosing the Spirit in a formulation, thus sharing in an attitude that has done much to diminish the living presence of the Spirit in the lives of men and women and in the common life of Christendom and the world that Christianity sanctifies. A more careful reading of the text shows that the Spirit initiates the whole process of Patrick's conversion and sanctification. In the second paragraph we read that in the state of captivity described in the first paragraph the Lord comes to Patrick: "And there the Lord opened up the feelings of my unbelieving heart so that I might at length remember my sins and turn with my whole heart to the Lord my God who had mercy on my youth and ignorance."

In this text two divine activities are clearly distinguished, the one coming from within and operating through the feelings (*sensus*), the other coming from above and bearing on Patrick's whole condition of helplessness and abjection. Now the second activity would not have found a point of entry to Patrick's consciousness had it not been preceded by the first: an "opening" was made, a rent in the tight cloak of incredulity, and through this aperture the light and warmth of God's merciful *and fatherly* love streams in, so that Patrick finds himself receiving strength and consolation as from a father towards his son. It is from this experience of the Father's presence and love that all else flows in Patrick's life of prayer and mission, and so the initiation of this process is the source and source-experience of all that Patrick is and does and stands for. Now this initiation is described in terms of two texts from the New Testament: Luke 24.45 and Hebrews 3.12. Both texts have to do with the opening of the heart to the words of Scripture, to the voice of God speaking through Scripture. In the first text Jesus opens the minds of his disciples to the Scriptures, and goes on to say that he is leaving them in order to send them the Holy Spirit by whom they will be clothed with power from on high (v. 49). There is nothing here about incredulity or sinfulness in the sense that Patrick intends; for this we have to go to the text in Hebrews where the main reference is to Psalm 95, that strange song of many voices that speak to man's hardness of heart in terms at once plaintive and comminatory: *Today, when you hear his voice do not harden your hearts as in the rebellion, in the day of testing in the wilderness* (Heb. 3.7 RSV). This text is quoted at some length by the author of Hebrews and is attributed to the Holy Spirit (v. 7). As it appears here in the Hebrews text it is the voice of the Holy Spirit telling of the voice of God which has spoken already in anger and wrought just retribution and is now speaking in accents of love and invitation — so it was that this Psalm became the Invitatory of the traditional *Officium Divinum* of the Church. Patrick, the sinner brought low, has lived the archetypal situation of this Scripture, and is thus led back to the Father's mercy. Ultimately the invitation to return comes from the Father, yet this invitation is conveyed by the Holy Spirit, who is also the Spirit of the Living God and the Spirit of the Father. We must step carefully and lightly here, for we are on holy ground. St. Paul tells us that it is through the Holy Spirit that we cry "Abba, Father" (Rom 7.15-16), and here at the beginning of Patrick's story we are dealing with a profound Abba-experience. We may ask: why does the Father not speak directly to the spirit of man? The answer seems to be that it is the Spirit of God that rightly speaks to the spirit of man, in accordance with St. Paul's mysterious statement: "No one knows a man's thoughts except the spirit of man which is in him. So also no one comprehends the thoughts of God except the Spirit of God" (1 Cor 2.11-12). We are in the world of intimacy here, of man's (and God's) inner conversation with himself. We are also in the world of man's (and God's?) loneliness. The Prodigal Son "sees", the face of his Father when he enters within his own spirit and takes a long look at himself. The Father's love has followed him all the way and now becomes *felt*, becomes a presence, a messenger that manifests itself in the light of the heart's deepest yearnings and pathos that had been occluded by the clouds of passion and presumption. It is an open question how far this kind of reflection is implied in Patrick's text at this point, but there is no doubt but that it expresses the situation expressed in the text. In the depths of his total loneliness, humiliation and despair, Patrick's spirit opens up to the Spirit of God that in turn reveals the face of eternal and all-fulfilling Fatherhood. Patrick's loneliness comes through in his words; deeper than Patrick's words yet surely not unfelt (for a text has a *feel* as well as a meaning) is the realisation of the Father's loneliness expressed in the deep-down stirring of the Holy Spirit within the human spirit.

We move on through one of Patrick's rare and beautiful exclamation-passages to his Rule of Faith, so-called, which begins with the Father, goes on to Jesus Christ as the Son "made man," and concludes with the Holy Spirit. Curiously, the Holy Spirit enters as a *flowing* that issues "abundantly" from Jesus Christ risen, ascended, and established as Judge of the living and the dead. This is not quite accurate, however.

For Patrick the Spirit flows, but he does not identify the Spirit with this flowing: there is room for the presupposition of the separate "centricity" and personhood of the Spirit. Yet we seem to be in a different world or area of discourse from that of the earlier part of this "Rule of Faith" paragraph, where the eternity and "substantiality" of the Father and Jesus Christ, His Son, are emphatically affirmed. By comparison the Spirit is seen in terms of relationship with man's needs and destiny. The Spirit is "the gift and pledge of immortality who makes those who receive and obey into Sons of God and sharers in the inheritance of Christ" (4). It is not that Patrick gives any real ground for the thesis that the Holy Spirit's full and equal divinity was a relatively late discovery (or invention).[12] Indeed he goes on to say that this same Spirit is "one God in the Trinity of the Sacred Name"; the Matthean Trinitarian formula is repeated explicitly later on (40) and equivalently not only here but towards the end of the *Confession* and as the closing valediction of the *Coroticus* letter. Even if we cannot dismiss these statements as perfunctory, it seems clear that for Patrick the Spirit is first and last a living companionable presence, so much so that there is a sense in which the *Confession* is the story of this companionship. In order to appreciate this we must return to Patrick's inner world of dreams and visions.

Perhaps the most extraordinary of Patrick's dream-visions or dream-auditions is that in which he finds somebody praying within him (25), a somebody first identified as Jesus Christ and then as the Spirit. Here, as in the missionary dream which called him back to Ireland, vision passes over into hearing, and a kind of conversation ensues in which the being who prays within Patrick reveals itself as the Spirit. But the core of the experience is deeper than speech uttered and heard. Patrick describes it as "sighs and groans" or rather as the hearing of these coming from the being who is praying within him. This causes Patrick (in his dream) the utmost astonishment, and it is then he asks who it can be. It would seem that

[12]On this question see J. P. Mackey, *The Christian Experience of God as Trinity*, (London, 1983), ch. 11.

this question is not answered immediately but only at the conclusion of the prayer when he is told that it is the Spirit. *Then* he awakens and recalls the text from St. Paul which says that the Spirit assists us in our inability to pray as we ought and "himself intercedes for us with sighs too deep for words" (Rom 8.26 RSV. The older versions had "unutterable groanings" which is more accurate). He also recalls another text, from the First Letter of St. John (2.1) which, for Patrick, reads: "The Lord our advocate prays for us."

The more I reflect on this dream-text the more I am held and astonished by it. Indeed I cannot think of any other text from the rich store of Christian witness which can compare with it for strangeness, intimacy and power. It is well to turn it round slowly to catch the light.

First, it is the account of a dream-experience, and this, apart from the general question of the significance of dreams in Christian doctrine and practice, has two special implications here: that the waking experience of which St. Paul speaks becomes realised in Patrick as a dream-experience, and secondly that the region of dreams has within it pathways along which the Holy Spirit can reach us. Both points affirm or postulate the enormous importance of what happens, or can happen, during sleep — or at least what happened or could happen at the time and in the milieu of the *Confession* of Patrick.

Secondly, as has been said, the story as Patrick tells it is a story of many voices. If we look closely we find a kind of Chinese box: on the outside there is the voice of Patrick the narrator, an old man separated from the experience itself by many years and a whole world of challenges and encounters, victories and defeats, continual meditation on the Gospel he preaches. In the face of all this the voice of Patrick telling his own story affirms the importance of this experience. It is not the voice of the morning after, sharing what the French call "a curiosity," but the voice of a man looking across a long vista and choosing what stands out most vividly and unforgettably. Inside there is the past voice of Patrick as he awakens from the dream and links it up with two New Testament texts, one obviously indicated by the very shape of the dream, the other rather unexpected and indeed somewhat disconcerting, as we shall see. Then there is the voice of Patrick *within* the dream questioning its meaning, and the voice (of the Spirit?) telling him that it is the Spirit who has been "speaking" within him. Finally there is this voice of the Spirit which is at the centre of the experience and which seems to have had two phases, one of "ordinary" praying and the other of inarticulate sighs and groans, though it seems clear that it is the inarticulate praying that is at the deepest centre of it all.

Thirdly, the dreamer is shown at two levels and as variously related to the being who is praying within him, the dreamer, who is in his body and hears the being who prays both as present within the body and as heard within the body. Yet what is heard from within the body, and *as* within the body, is at the same time "above the inner man." Patrick has the sense of being himself (in the dream) and thus within his own body, yet a whole inner world "appears" within, a world of the Spirit, of Patrick's own spirit and the Holy Spirit that speaks (inarticulately) within him. It may be said that there is question of an epiphany within a dream, but we say this at the risk of diminishing the force of the epiphany, the sheer impact of an experience which clearly is not only not forgotten but is unforgettable. Make of it what we can, we are forced to recognise that most of the peaks of awareness in Patrick's life (as he looks back) belong to the world of dreams.

Fourthly and finally, this text seems at one and the same time to identify and distinguish Christ and the Holy Spirit. This becomes evident as we try to answer the question: who or what is the being who speaks within the dreamer? We know that Patrick himself asks this question (within the dream) and is given a clear answer: it is the Spirit. This would seem to solve the question, but it does not. For Patrick the narrator begins the account by saying that it was Christ, *He who has given his life for you* (24), who was praying within, and again, at the end, the text he quotes from *1 John* refers unambiguously to Christ as "our advocate with the Father." On the other hand the text from St. Paul refers unambiguously to the Holy Spirit. Obviously Patrick, following St. Paul, can speak of the Holy Spirit as the Spirit of Christ (20), but the question has to be faced as to the personal or hypostatic (i.e., substantial) separateness of the Holy Spirit not only in relation to Christ but also in relation to the Father. I have argued above that the texts from the New Testament in which Patrick tells of his conversion towards God the Father are Spirit texts, yet it cannot be said that Patrick is speaking of a separate person or centre of activity: the most that can be said is that there is question of the Spirit of the Father as intimately in touch with the heart of the lonely and humiliated adolescent placed suddenly in the position of the Prodigal Son. The presence of the Spirit seems to be simply a special presence of the Father.

So, too, in the Satan-encounter, where Patrick is paralysed by the great rock that falls on him, or rather that something that falls on him *like* a great rock (20). He emerges from this terror crying out "Elias, Elias," and then the Christ-sun rises in the heavens. "And I knew," Patrick continues, "that I was helped by Christ the Lord and that His Spirit was already at that time crying out on my behalf." It seems as if the presence of the Spirit here also is simply the presence of Christ, the Lord: there is no question, it would seem, of a separate person or personality.

On the other hand there are the Trinitarian formulae set down twice in the *Confession* and once in *Coroticus*. Are these formulae in Patrick's day merely credal and liturgical, repeating a tradition that goes back to a one-off statement in the Gospels (Matt 28.19) without any real implication of the full and separate personhood of the Holy Spirit? To deal fairly with this question in the context of the *Confession* it is best to aproach Patrick's witness to the Holy Spirit from a fresh standpoint.

5

The Indwelling Spirit

In Patrick's understanding of the Trinity, God the Father is above and beyond all man's days and ways, yet not at all alien or unapproachable; there is nothing nearer to the son than his Father's countenance. Yet the Father shines downwards from above as the son, in the totality of his being, looks upward. It is a face to face relationship and to that extent concrete, external, embodied in creation and creaturehood. As described in the Rule of Faith, Jesus Christ is also above and beyond all that is merely human; as Christ is discovered in Patrick's experience, however, he is a friend, companion and fellow-sufferer who describes himself as the one who has given his own soul for his friend. Here we have passed inwards into the world of the soul, the *anima* or life-principle. This is the world of feeling, of tears and yearnings, of hope and consolation, the world of friendship where heart speaks to heart. Patrick would have understood perfectly what came later to be known as Devotion to the Heart of Jesus Christ and would have approved all that one of his spiritual descendants, Columba Marmion, was to say in his great book, *Christ, the Life of the Soul*.[13] Patrick read the Old and New Testa-

[13] *Le Christ, vie de L'Ame*, Maredsous: Belgium, 1918: Eng. translation, London, 1922.

ments with the eyes of the heart, and in communion with the Holy Spirit.

Now the place where Patrick meets the Holy Spirit is in the depths of his own spirit. If the Father is above him and Jesus Christ beside him, the Spirit is within him. The Spirit, for Patrick, is in the inner sanctuary of the soul, what a later mystical tradition was to call "the cell of self-knowledge." It is here, and not in the world of concrete objects, that the Holy Spirit is a substantial, self-subsistent, individual entity. It is from within that the Spirit reveals itself and operates. It is through the Spirit that the Father and the Son make intimate contact and conversation with the human spirit. Thus it is that the Spirit is the Spirit of the Father and equally the Spirit of the Son. Since Father and Son are distinct "in the unity of the Sacred Name," so the Spirit, belonging equally to each, is not to be identified with the one or the other. But this kind of observation is no more than a bare logical implication unless we give it its own soil and habitation in the human spirit. The Spirit can be known only where it dwells or rather where it lives and grows.

There is one phrase in the *Confession* which shows us this process in its happening. Patrick is talking, in a very eloquent passage, of his way of life as he tended his master's flocks in the days of his servitude and humiliation. Nothing of all this hardship seemed to matter, for he had found his heavenly companionship, so that his whole life was one long prayer. It was the time of "first favours," to use once again a later terminology. It was also the time of the Spirit's first burgeoning within Patrick's spirit. "In those days," he tells us, "the spirit was on fire within me" (16). As the text stands the spirit in question here is Patrick's own spirit, yet some translators — Bishop Philbin for example — have taken spirit to mean the Holy Spirit by giving it a capital letter. It seems to me that here as elsewhere in the *Confession* the human spirit is understood as the place of inhabitation and growth of the Spirit of God. In this particular text which tells of a fire in the human spirit we are in the world of the "flame of living love" of St. John of the Cross. John tells us that this flame that "wounds the soul in its inmost depth" is in fact, and not simply by way of analogy or metaphor, the Holy Spirit. [14] Patrick does not have the poetic or theological resources of the Mystical Doctor, yet he expresses a no less intense experience in simple and memorable language.

The spirit in man and woman, the human spirit, that is, is inner dialogue and reflection; it is the place or centre where the *I am* that I am affirms itself as "I am." It is that most secret and sacred centre of my ownmost self, the place of what is sometimes called "the fundamental option," that initial and determinative option for good or evil, for giving or taking, for truth or deception, for life or death. But deeper than this decison is what is called the voice of conscience, which is also the voice of the Spirit of God speaking, as our greatest modern philosopher saw, categorically. This voice is the voice of Psalm 95, the voice that Patrick heard in the time of his humiliation and desperation. This voice, he came to recognise, is the voice of the Holy Spirit. Out of the ardent kindling of love the voice of the Spirit began to find articulation through the world of dreams, at that threshold or vestibule between sleeping and waking where the human spirit is totally alone in the world of spirits. The place or region of physical awakening became the ground of those spiritual awakenings of which the mystical tradition speaks, awakenings to the call of love to do and to suffer, to approach the portals of total dedication, of total self-giving, of the full following of Jesus Christ all the way to Calvary and the Resurrection. So it was that Patrick speaks of being "bound by the spirit" (43) as St. Paul was (Acts 20.22-23).

The Spirit within his spirit binds Patrick to his mission as well as assuring him of support and consolation. Through the Spirit Patrick is also held more deeply bound into the unity of the Trinity. This is not a union in which he loses himself or in which the distinctiveness of the Father and the Son disappears. "Union differentiates," says Teilhard de Chardin, clearly enunciating for the first time the central principle of Trinitarian theology. The more deeply the Father enters into

[14]See *The Living Flame of Love* Stanza 1, Par 2. (p. 580 in the *Collected Works of St. John of the Cross*, tr. by Kavanaugh and Rodriguez, Washington, 1979).

union with the Son the more the Father is Father, and the more the Son is affirmed in the relation of Sonship. So, too, the Holy Spirit becomes more fully itself according as it loses itself in the immense conflagration of the creative union of the Source and the all-mirroring beauty and glory of Jesus Christ. Patrick knows that the Holy Spirit brings all heaven as a free gift to his spirit, and his Rule of Faith bends strongly in this direction at the point where the Holy Spirit is introduced. The Spirit is "the gift and pledge of immortal life making us Sons of God and sharers in the inheritance of Christ" (4).

For Patrick everything good that is shown forth in his life and actions is a gift of God (*Donum Dei*) and comes by divine favor (*gratia*). Nevertheless there does not seem to be any clear concept of created grace in the *Confession*. All is gift, but there is no special gift that can be called "grace" in the Augustinian sense. For St. Augustine and the theologians who followed him grace was understood as an entity or force or influence that effected justification, regeneration, transformation, even deification. The sinful human was somehow taken over by this divine force, so much so that man's freedom of choice was sometimes reduced to a shadowy power of acquiescence or declared to be totally corrupt. So it came about that the question of the relative force of God's grace (governing man's destiny to the extent of predestination) and man's freedom to reject this grace or co-operate with it, to "merit" it or be simply given or refused it according to God's unfathomable design, became the central question of Christian theology. Patrick's *Confession* seems to know nothing of this controversy. In place of a doctrine of created grace Patrick has a doctrine of the uncreated spirit. In place of a confrontation of two agencies, divine grace and human freedom, we find an intimate conversation of two spirits, the spirit of man and the Holy Spirit of God. The freedom that is present, and this is *totally* present, is the freedom that forms the atmosphere of intimate love. Looking at his life from the outside, in the world of men and events, Patrick insists that all is gift, all is favour. But when he looks within, what is present and operative is his soul-companionship with Jesus Christ and his spirit-companionship with the Holy Spirit. God's gift is God's presence graciously given and graciously received. Throughout all Patrick's references to the Divine presence and presences there is a sense of delicacy, intimacy and vulnerability, and a real companionship in suffering as Patrick contends with the opposition of demons and men, as he experiences a whole new world coming to birth within himself and emerging from the mysterious womb of sleep. At times it seems as if Patrick's soul and spirit were merely the ground of a mighty struggle of light against darkness, yet this ground is living and personal and filled with Patrick's deep strong sense of selfhood and individual pathos.

St. Thomas describes the indwelling of the Holy Spirit in the human soul as that of the Lover in the Beloved.[15] Patrick assumes a distinction between soul and spirit which gives this statement a deeper poignancy. It is at the very centre of his selfhood, in the most intimate conversation of his heart that he encounters the Spirit of God, the Eternal Spirit dwelling within the human spirit. It would seem that for Patrick it is the Holy Spirit that brings to the human spirit the gift of immortality. This does not seem to involve the taking up of a definite position against the thesis of the survival of natural man which St. Augustine and his contemporaries received from Greek philosophy and which (arguably) is reflected in the New Testament, but is rather a deep existential sense of human finitude and human vulnerability to the forces of annihilation. Like every reflective person Patrick carried a philosophy around with him but it was largely unexamined. In other words, he was not a philosopher after the manner of St. Augustine or St. Thomas Aquinas.

[15]*S. Theol.* I, Q 43 art. 3.

6

The Dark Angel

Patrick's terrifying night-experience of being, as it were, paralysed by a mighty power "like a huge rock" falling on him remained deeply written in his memory, and in this sense never left him. We do not know whether the same experience returned from time to time, but it is clear that it was always with him, as a repeatable possibility arising from his very depths, and thus, in the strict sense, existential. It opened up within his spirit a deep, indeed a measureless abyss of fear, helplessness and loneliness, and there was absolutely nothing he could do to prevent it from pressing in on him again.

In fact Patrick makes it clear that he knows he will have to face this terror again; perhaps he recalled the chilling phrase from Luke's account of the encounter of Jesus Christ with the Angel of Darkness to the effect that Satan "left him for a while," or, as the NEB puts it, "departed, biding his time" (4.13). For, of course, Patrick is quite clear that this was a visitation from Satan, and we can assume that he was not confusing it with any of the more ordinary fears and nightmares that surround the portals of sleep. For it must be noted that Patrick is not recounting an experience which he *interprets* as Satanic, rather is he telling us of what comes to him as a very concrete encounter. The text has the same quality of

immediacy as that in which St. Paul speaks of being buffeted
by an Angel of Satan (2 Cor 12.7). In both accounts there is a
strong sense of the concrete presence of a powerful adversary,
so powerful indeed that man is defenceless before it. Paul
cried out "three times" to be delivered from this enemy, and
his request is refused in the terms in which he made it (12.8
and 9). He was told that he had to remain vulnerable and
helpless in face of this strong adversary, since the grace of God
was sufficient for him (12.9).
  Patrick does not cry out to be delivered, yet it is clear that
the Dark Angel was never far away. Like St. Paul he has to
live in hope, in a total confidence that he will be given the help
he needs in "the time of trial," when again he will have to face
the same adversary. He does not however talk of grace but
rather of the Holy Spirit. When the sun of Christ rises to
deliver him he realises that he has been helped by the Holy
Spirit within, the Spirit that prompted him to cry out "Helia,
Helia" with all his strength.
  It is easy to miss the power and subtlety of the *Confession*
narrative at this point. What he is saying is that he was
delivered from Satan because he was led to cry out, so that it is
that which led him to cry out which is the real helper. For it is
within his own human spirit that the terror and paralysis
moves in to destroy him, and it is within this same spirit that
comfort arises and opens up towards the vision of the Christ-
splendour. It is precisely because of this that he is able to
speak of hope, the hope that "in the day of trial" he will
likewise be saved by the Holy Spirit of Christ. The delicate,
and not always appreciated point here, for both Paul and
Patrick, is that the divine help is entirely absent until the time
comes when it is needed. This absence is at the very centre of
the attitude or virtue of hope: "We hope for what we do not
see" (Rom 8.25). What Patrick has is the memory of what was
done in him by the Holy Spirit in the past, and it is precisely
this memory that is the ground of the hope that he will be
provided for in the future. This may seem a tenuous ground
for hope, as if it were to depend on the possession of a
sufficiently good memory. Yet it is in the memory and only in
the memory that the Gospel promises have their home, and

what is in question here, as elsewhere in facing things, is human consciousness not only as facing forward but also as looking back. To live in hope is to bring the past along with us into the future. It is a dynamic living process. To live only in the past is to fail to face the challenge of a world in the making; to live only in the future is to be involved in constant care and concern, to carry each day the burden of the morrow. Patrick is a man of action who fares forward all the time, but he carries along with him the remembrance of God's power and intimate presence, so that he can look all human and demonic enemies in the face. Yet this kind of statement gives a false impression, for Patrick was never without fear: a deep anxiety runs right through the *Confession*. Indeed it could be said that both the *Confession* and the *Coroticus* letter are different manifestations of Patrick's cares, fears and anxieties. The holy superman described in the "lives" of Patrick is nowhere to be found in Patrick's own writings.

Patrick is full of fear, but he is also full of love, a love that belongs and overbalances the fear, but never neutralises it. Love does indeed cast out each fear as it tries to take over, and it may be said that the whole movement of Patrick's life is towards that fulness of love that casts out all fear (1 Jn 4.18), but Patrick is too constantly involved in the conflict between light and darkness to be for long without "fear and trembling." He does indeed look his enemies, both human and demonic, in the face, but he remains a very vulnerable human being, a man of fears and tears.

So there is much poignancy and pathos in those passages in the *Confession* where Patrick affirms his hope and confidence that all will be well. The recalling of God's favours is not only a duty of gratitude but also an affirmation of that hope which for St. John of the Cross has its dwelling-place in the memory. As he looks back Patrick sees his enemies and the Archenemy that would oppress him totally. But he also sees that Triune presence, sees it in its unity but also in its trinity, the Father raising him, the Son sharing agony and glory with him, the Holy Spirit speaking deep within him. It is the Holy Spirit especially that lives in his memory as his companion in the deep dark places of annihilation and despair. He did not, however, possess this Spirit as a constant comforting presence; rather did he reach outwards through remembered goodness to future goodness not yet realised. In the everyday it seems likely that the writer of the *Confession* lived in the absence of all spiritual comfort. This does not mean the absence of joy but the presence of both joy and sorrow, of consolation and desolation, in that "doubling" of the soul spoken of by some of the mystics.[16]

There opens up here a mighty world of spiritual experience which is not dimmed but rather manifested by the plain and ragged language in which the experience is clothed. In the genesis of this experience the Dark Angel is, in the last analysis, the servant of the divine purposes, bringing Patrick to that paradoxical hope which arise from contention with despair, that hope in which the human spirit has to let go entirely and yield place to the Spirit of God. The letting go is only total if the Spirit has not yet come, and is left totally free to come or not to come. All is given; all is lost; all is found.

---

[16]The mystic who most clearly expresses this phenomenon of the simultaneous presence of joy and sorrow in the spirit is Sr. Angeles Sorazu, the Basque Franciscan (1873–1921). See P. L. Villasante, *M. Angeles Sorazu*, Desclee de Brouwer, Bilbao, 1950. The Spanish term is *desdoblamiento* which I translate as "doubling." See also Book 7 of St. Teresa's *Interior Castle*.

7

Mission and Memory

There is a popular impression, enshrined in some of the less scholarly presentations of the text, that the *Confession* was addressed to Patrick's Irish converts. This impression is contrary not only to the whole tone of the book, and to the fact that it was written in Latin (not the language of his converts), but to Patrick's own explicit statement of his aim. This aim is in the first instance "to reveal and confess the works of God," in accordance with the injunction of the Archangel Raphael in the Book of Tobias (accepted by Patrick as Holy Writ). But in the second instance it has a very definite purpose expressed clearly and carefully. "Even though I am in many things imperfect, yet I wish my brethren and my own family (*cognati*) to know what manner of man I am, that they may see clearly why I have chosen to do what I have done" (6). It is because he is addressing it to people of a certain degree of cultivation that Patrick is so painfully apologetic about his "rusticity" and lack of polish. Besides, the author of the *Confession* is clearly a man under attack, clearly a man who wants to clear up misunderstandings, clearly a man facing the judgement of his peers as well as the demands of proud kinsfolk that he should be seen to have acted honorably, especially in financial matters (48, 49).

Nevertheless Patrick does not rule out the fact that what he is writing is part of the heritage which he leaves behind him to his Irish converts, indeed to what can only be seen as a new church that has emerged from his ministry: "My brothers (and sisters) and my children (men and women) many thousands of them" (14). All his experiences, all the fervor and power that flows out from his early mystical awakenings in his time of slavery, all his dreams and visions, all that he has received from Christ as call and sending forth (40, 43): all that he is and does and receives flows out towards "that people of God which he has found and established at the world's end" (58).

Yet for all his many references to the mission he has received from Christ, Patrick tells us little or nothing about his missionary work in Ireland in its day-to-day journeyings and encounters. Not once does he mention a single Irish convert by name, though some of them must have been people of social and political importance being "the sons and daughters of chieftains" (41). The author of the *Confession* was clearly a very person-oriented man, and what we know of the Ireland of his day reveals a very individualistic people (as, of course, the Irish still are), yet the whole account of Patrick's mission is shrouded in impersonality.

This impersonality is partly, though not fully, explained by the fact that the *Confession* looks at mission and apostleship from the viewpoint of its source rather than of its manifestation. It is mainly the source of his ministry that has been put in question, and this is nowhere fully resolved *at the ecclesial level* in the *Confession*. Of course subsequent "lives" of Patrick provided more than ample evidence of an ecclesial sending, from the Church in Britain or in Gaul or by a direct commission from Rome. All we know from the *Confession* itself is that Patrick was at some stage, however grudgingly or even ambiguously, appointed a bishop (26 to 33), and it is safe to assume even as early as the fifth century an ecclesial structure and ambience for this appointment. Beyond this we cannot go.

What is abundantly clear from the *Confession* is that Patrick has received repeatedly a direct call from God to bring the Christian message to Ireland. He is his own man, and he goes his own way following his own dreams and divine "responses," and in all this his little book remains a challenge to structure and institution and to all that his Roman background demands of him as regards law and order and ordinance. And we know that the Church which he established went its own way for centuries until it was finally broken in and brought into line with the Roman centre.

There are wide and thorny questions here, and I want to stay within the limits of the text. Patrick does indeed go his own way and claims his own source of illumination, yet he is deeply and painfully anxious to be accepted in himself and in his mission by his brethren and family, who, it would seem, stand for the universal Church. Clearly the one thing he wants to avoid is that these people won so marvellously for Christ "at the world's end" should be isolated from the Christian mainland. It is perhaps this anxiety most of all that led him to undertake the (for him) laborious task of writing the *Confession,* and it is this anxiety that gives it its inner tension and pathos. This tension is creative, full of a great new people of God being born; this pathos is the very pulse of fatherhood: here again, the comparison with St. Paul imposes itself as we recall how Paul's texts dissolve in tenderness and tears when he expresses his father-relationship with those he has "begotten in Christ" (1 Cor 4.14, 15). I want to look more closely in turn at this creative tension and fatherly pathos.

The sense of tension is everywhere in the *Confession* from the first sentence to the last. Patrick begins by telling the reader that he is a sinner at once unlettered and contemptible — the description goes far beyond the conventional pious expressions of humility and disclaimers of personal merit. This is one pole of tension that comes up again and again, that in fact never resolves itself or leaves off. Now here already in this very first sentence Patrick begins to build up the other pole of the tension by telling his readers that he comes of ancient and well-regarded Christian stock. He is what is called in Scotland "a son of the manse," indeed is a third-generation son of the manse, as so many great Scottish missionaries have been over the centuries. So, his "rusticity" is balanced by his heredity; he is not a nobody, not just Magunios, the Pigman, as his detractors named him. From this base Patrick is able to build up a likely story of conversion and divine favours, all of which more and more pulls against the strong and repeated admission of his lack of learning, lack of elegance as a writer and lack of theological training and competence.

Patrick's obvious lack of stylistic polish allows him to use, consciously or unconsciously, a very powerful rhetorical strategem, that of taking an accusation to its limits and beyond and using it precisely to accentuate its polar opposite. He goes the whole way and beyond with those who treat him with contempt because of his lack of all that is thought to befit a Christian bishop and thus allows full scope to what has been given him as *Donum Dei,* divine favour. It is on this note precisely that the *Confession* ends. There is indeed at the end a kind of resolution of the tension between Patrick's own little-ness and the greatness of what he has been given from above: "It was not my ignorance that did this work; rather it is a gift of God" (62). At this point the pole of Patrick's ignorance has been totally absorbed by the pole of the Divine Will and generosity, as its proper human correlative, at once passive and receptive. All the glory is given to God but Patrick's rusticity has been the human mirror of this glory.

Now the Irish mission emerges as the creative release and resolution of this polar tension. It is precisely because of Patrick's littleness and rusticity that God has been able to work this mighty work of conversion against all the odds. In this birthing of a new people of God, Patrick is by no means a purely negative condition or occasion. All he has suffered, all that he has personally received in his times of sleep as well as in his waking — all this is the necessary ground or womb of what is being born. Patrick's inner being is the womb of the Irish Church, and the story of his mystical love and mission-ary travails is the story of a new world being conceived and born. Patrick is at once father and mother of this new crea-tion, yet if we are to understand receptivity as the mother's way, then Patrick is more mother than father. It is true that for every man the mystical is the opening up of "the other side" of his nature, the feminine, and this is especially clear in Patrick's case, for his young manhood has had to face the terrible total fall into slavery. Through this experience he could have hardened into bitterness or self-destruction as could also the Prodigal Son of the parable. In the one case as in the other manhood was achieved by way of the emergence of the other side, the feminine.

Part of this balance of forces within the human personality is a sense of compassion, a compassion at once tender and practical. Compassion in the heart of man and woman is a sharing in the Divine compassion, and it opens out to infinite horizons. But there is something else in the full and flowing human heart that is special to man and woman and is surely the crowning beauty of the complete man as of the complete woman. This is pathos, that central human mystery which is the very stuff of poetry, yet which neither philosophy nor theology has as yet explored or even recognised. Pathos has to do with the vanishing of human endeavor, the vanishing of the significance and preciousness conferred on things and events by the living breath of the human spirit. The garden that was so hopefully tended, the hat worn with a flourish, the walking-stick: all are centres of pathos now that my friend has died and all those ardent concerns are no more.[17]

One catches the note of pathos everywhere in the *Confession,* in the flow of the narrative, in certain phrases that form a kind of structure of refrains, above all in the cadences of the words:

> *Ego Patricius peccator*
> *rusticissimus et*
> *minimus omnium fidelium*
> *et contemtibillisimus*
> *apud plurimos...*

[17]I have attempted an analysis of Pathos as a theological and mystical concept in two chapters of *Heaven in Ordinarie* (T and T Clark, 1979). It seems to me that this aspect of the human-divine relationship has been almost totally neglected by theologians. Its acceptance and incorporation in systematic theology would, it seems to me, revolutionise both the mind and praxis of the Christian Church.

To read these words slowly and to listen to their cadences is to encounter a spirit that is the very breath of pathos, and to know that exile has opened up into a larger home-world which the writer sees already vanishing as he writes his "Confession before I die." Pathos has its home in the memory: it may be called the lamp that lights up the house of memory and all within this house that is familiar, fragile, cherished, built up however uncertainly against the chaos and darkness all around. In the gentle cadences of the *Confession* one may hear, if one listens to such things, Patrick's lament for his lost childhood, the unassuageable pain of exile. But there is also the now familiar world of his Irish Christian family and all its familiarities, and the poignant realisation that this too is fragile and transient. One small and curious phrase binds the two worlds together: *tot millia hominum*, literally "so many thousand people." Patrick was taken into slavery with *tot millia hominum* (1); in turn he had gained for Christ *tot millia hominum* (14, 50). A world lost, a world gained: the one as fragile as the other; thus one hears that rise and fall of a phrase that has more inner significance than external meaning.

If pathos dwells in the memory so also does hope, hope not as a feeling arising from temperament or good fortune, but as a deep attitude towards reality as ultimate and unbounded horizon, in other words, towards God. Pathos casts its gentle and glowing light on the evanescence of all that is familiar and cherished and dearly purchased in the coin of the realm of the heart and its wonders. It is an evening radiance, varied and beautiful as the colors of sunset. Hope brings the Most High God into this vanished and vanishing world, rather does it accept this presence in some or all of its remembered presences: from one point of view, perhaps the most complete, Patrick's *Confession* like Augustine's is an expression of remembered Divine Presence and presences, especially (in Patrick's case) of the Holy Spirit of God within the anxious and oppressed spirit of man. In this perspective the sunset colors of pathos become mingled with the first streaks of dawn after the manner of midsummer in the far north of Scotland, not yet the land of the midnight sun but the nearby land of the midnight sunset passing over into the midnight sunrise.

Yet this image will not do, for the nature of hope is to possess the future not as present but as absent. What is present is the remembrance of God's love and care, in Patrick's case, of the Spirit's breathings within him, a voice deeper than all articulate words, more powerful than the terrors and paralysing power of Satan. This presence-in-absence of the Holy Spirit allows the human spirit to open up to the sunset colours of human pathos so as to bring this glory with it fully absorbed so that the new heavens is also a new earth. That is the most profound meaning of saying that a work like the *Confession* is immortal. The script we read is but the partial and inadequate presentation of the script written in the memory where pathos and hope mingle in the light of eternal love.

8

Man and Woman

Patrick's *Confession* is at first sight a very masculine document. In naming his family background he tells us he is the son of Calpornius and the grandson of Potitus, but there is not a word about his mother. His theology seems to ignore the presence of Mary in the Incarnation, though he does at one point mention Mary's Magnificat, yet without naming Mary (12). What seems to come across all through is the portrait of a man who moves always among men, and who keeps himself at a severe distance from women and the feminine.

There is, however, a paragraph towards the end of the *Confession* which puts this first impression very definitely in question. Suddenly, dramatically even, a woman steps into the narrative, a woman who is at once beautiful, and of noble family (as was Patrick himself). Not just beautiful, *pulchra*, but of surpassing beauty, *pulcherrima* (42). He does not give her a name, for the *Confession* names nobody but Patrick himself, so we can perhaps call her Pulcherrima.

Patrick tells us that he himself baptized Pulcherrima. This would have been a very real bond at both the physical and the spiritual level, for baptism in those days was by total immersion after the manner of Baptist baptism today, no less decorous, one may surmise, but for all that a very physical event, a

washing of the whole body from which Pulcherrima would
have emerged radiant in a white garment. It is difficult in our
day of infant baptism and the mere pouring of water across
the infant's forehead (at which the infant not infrequently
protests vigorously) to visualise the great and inspiring event
that Baptism was in early centuries, not only for the baptizand
but also for the community and those looking in from outside. It was surely an experience of radiance and glory not
easily forgotten.

Patrick baptized thousands, he tells us (14), baptized them
personally as he travelled around Ireland (*ego baptizavi*)
creating an ever-increasing procession of whiterobed men and
women. In describing this procession in *Coroticus*, Patrick
allows himself a moment of poetry, rare in the *Confession*,
rarer still in *Coroticus*: "their foreheads were bright with the
fragrance of their anointing" (*Cor* 3). These are the neo-
phytes, "the newly illumined ones," and they provide the
centre of significance of Patrick's whole missionary endeav-
our, which thus appears as light and fragrance continually
renewing itself.

Within this radiant and joyful procession there are some in
whom the new light shines forth with special clarity, and
whose whole life opens up to the anointing and the fragrance
of baptism. These are the monks and virgins, for the most
part, it would seem, sons and daughters of the chieftains (41).
And it is within this most radiant and devoted group that
Pulcherrima appears and seems suddenly and strangely to
stand beside Patrick himself as his partner and companion.
She had received baptism, Patrick tells us, and returned to her
own home, and then after a few days came back "for a special
reason" (*una causa*). She came to tell of an experience in
which a "divine messenger" (*Dei nuntius*) had told her that
she should become a "virgin of Christ" and so come closer to
God. After six days she obeyed this call perfectly and fer-
vently and thus became part of a great movement of women
vowed to virginity or to widowhood or continence (*viduae et
continentes*).

This simple story has several points of significance. In the
first place, Pulcherrima meets with an angel, and Patrick

accepts this without question as part of Christian experience. There may be some ground, then, for the tradition that Patrick was conscious of constant angelic guidance. Indeed he tells us that his *Confession* is made "in the sight of God and his holy angels" (61). We know that the presence of angels was commonly and constantly recognised in the Irish Church after Patrick, as in all Celtic Christianity all through the centuries right up to the present day and its last surviving remnants. Pulcherrima is not seen by Patrick as a woman who has a kind of experience common in *women*; rather is she seen as a *Christian* who is accorded a special privilege. Secondly, this experience culminates in a *responsum*, and this term links this woman's experience with Patrick's experiences of divine guidance which are seen also as *responsa*. A *responsum* is not so much a response as a divine message — so Duffy translates — or intimation. It is a term that indicates a special divine intimacy, as a moment within an ongoing dialogue of the human spirit with the Spirit of God, and apart from Patrick himself nobody else is favoured with this experience in the course of the *Confession*. Thirdly , the entry of Pulcherrima into his life is remembered by Patrick after many years with circumstantial accuracy: she returns *a few days* after baptism and makes her commitment to Christian virginity *six days* after that. This bright vision of radiant and devout womanhood entered deeply into Patrick's consciousness.

Was Patrick disturbed or troubled at this admittedly attractive feminine presence? In the immediate context of Pulcherrima's story he goes on to talk in general terms of his own calling as a missioner far from his own country and family, and of troublesome desires within the flesh "that always lead towards death." He puts this down to his own past sinfulness. Like the "sinfulness" of the young Augustine Patrick's "past sinfulness" seems to be no more than the story of the normal growth to adulthood of a youth of lively and passionate temperament, yet in Patrick's narrative there is not any trace of that sense of radical and all-pervasive guilt that characterises Augustine's account of himself. There is indeed an extraordinary and refreshing innocence about Pulcherrima's entry into the narrative. She could not have thus entered Augustine's narrative in *his* account of his experiences in the *Confession*. Her presence may have troubled Patrick, but it did not scare him or force him to denigrate, distort or "demonise" her bright feminine reality. She has a right to be Pulcherrima.

It is clear that Pulcherrima in making her commitment to virginity and the search for divine union found herself part of a large and growing movement of dedicated women, not only young unwed women like herself but also widows and *continentes*. This latter group were married women who followed St. Paul's injunction to live as if they were free of marriage, presumably by agreement with convert husbands, or else because they had left their husbands. Questions arise here which I do not feel equipped to follow up, historical questions which, as far as I know, historians have not explored in any detail. All that can be said is that Patrick names three groups of women who led lives of total dedication according to some kind of vow of chastity.

There were, of course, the men as well, the monks, *monachi*, and the clerks whom Patrick ordained; presumably ordained clerics could also be monks. It would seem from the *Confession* that Patrick went around baptizing and ordaining and also creating communities of monks and virgins. But neither the *Confession* nor *Coroticus* give us any real information as to how these religious communities were organised. It is difficult to escape the impression that Patrick found some kind of monastic structure already in operation, and that he was content to work within this. We know that in the early Church men and women worked closely together (this is clear from St. Paul's First Letter to the Corinthians) and Patrick's account of his mission seems a kind of continuation or return to this; indeed every upsurge of Christian consciousness seems to produce a re-enactment of this first innocence of holy living which loses its power and freshness as the movement becomes organised and self-conscious. At any rate, at the level of personal impression, I find that the *Confession* in this and other matters gives a strong impression of first fervour and first innocence, qualities that are indeed very vulnerable, yet qualities also without which religion cannot survive for long.

Patrick brings under one heading monks and virgins of Christ, but there is no doubt as to which group is the nearer to his heart. Not only are the virgins mentioned more frequently than the monks (who are never mentioned separately), not only is the story of Pulcherrima without a masculine parallel, but there is a special warmth and concern in the case of the virgins which is clearly evident in three instances. Firstly, there is the matter of opposition from parents and masters which goes as far as persecution and insults, and is especially heavy in the case of those women who share Patrick's own former condition of slavery (41). Second, there is the question of the gifts which these women placed on the altar, their personal ornaments, which they freely gave to Patrick as Christ's representative, and which Patrick insisted on giving back to them again lest his ministry be prejudiced (49). Clearly this caused real hurt and misunderstanding, and clearly Patrick is deeply sensitive to this: it remains as a wound in his heart as if he is conscious that he has acted ungraciously. Thirdly, and tragically, we see Patrick's agony concerning those dedicated women who have been captured by Coroticus and are at the disposal of pagan masters (*Cor* 12 and 14).

It is clear that the man who wrote the *Confession* and *Coroticus* is deeply and sensitively open to women and womanhood, and has in himself a certain vulnerability, if not a susceptibility, which nevertheless does not take refuge in a grim and pretentious asceticism, nor yet in that neurotic fear of and contempt for the feminine which has entered so deeply into the attitudes and structures of the Christian Church in its main manifestations. In this respect he is a complete man.

9

The End of the World

The *Confession* is an account of new beginnings, of a whole people brought into the Christian fold, of a new world opening up. For us today it is not only a source book but a dawn book, the first grey dawn and the first touches of sunrise. It is therefore something of a shock to realise that what the author feels he is presenting is an account of the end of the world. This belief arises from the conjunction of certain scriptural texts with what the author took to be a plain fact of geographical observation.

A whole sheaf of end-of-the-world texts may be easily garnered from the Bible, and we find Patrick doing just this in the latter part of the *Confession*. Perhaps the most pointed of these texts is Matthew 24.14, where Jesus replies to the question of the time of the end-of-the-world by saying that the Gospel must first be preached throughout the whole world as a testimony to all nations, "and then the end will come" (40, 34). In Patrick's time this text was taken to mean that the end of the world would come as soon as the Gospel had been preached to all nations of the world as far as the extreme borders of the inhabited earth.

Now Patrick was convinced that his own journeying as a herald of the Gospel had taken him to this far borderland of the world. And so we find this remarkable gloss on the text from Matthew. "This text has been fulfilled; for behold, we are witnesses to the fact that the Gospel has been preached in those regions beyond which no man dwells" (34). It is perhaps significant that this gloss, like the account of Pulcherrima, has been omitted from the text of the *Confession* found in the Book of Armagh: Patrick is there presented not only as far above any noticing of feminine beauty but also as free of dubious prophesying.

Patrick was of course writing at the time of the break-up of the Roman Empire, and he must have absorbed some of that sense of a world grown old and in the process of dissolution that led St. Augustine to write *The City of God*. He was a man of his time writing for the men of his time. Indeed the fact that he defends his mission in this way — as an indication that the end is near — shows how deep was this sense of the end of the world among Patrick's contemporaries. This was clearly compounded by a strong assumption that Ireland, or at least those parts of Ireland farthest from Britain, was a barbarous and godless region, at the far limit of possibility as regards human habitation. This was perhaps essential to the northerly British in order to affirm their own identity as part of a civilised world that had its near centre in Gaul and its far centre in Rome. It is clear in any case, from both the *Confession* and *Coroticus*, that for Patrick and his own people Ireland was an alien land, and it is hard to escape the impression that this sense of strangeness sometimes ascending towards wonder (admiration in its original Latin sense) sometimes descending towards contempt, still remains somewhere in the soil of the larger of the Isles of the North. And of course this has its response in feelings and attitudes in the smaller island.

All this is speculation (though I do not think it should be lightly dismissed) and our concern is with the *text* of the *Confession*. The end-of-the-world theme is there, no doubt about that, but it is all the same a minor theme. The *Confession* is not a Doomsday tract. Rather is it full of hope and aspiration even within the horizons of the pilgrim church. The world opened up in Patrick's dreams is a world full of hope, full of the future. Even when he speaks of his trials and difficulties and of his "rusticity" and inadequacy the atmosphere is never one of doom and guilt. In his six years as a slave, tending cattle and entering into the realities and changes of the elements, Patrick had learned the feel of things and the solidity of the earth. His acceptance of the end-of-the-world theology did not strike deep roots in him. Nevertheless it is there in the *Confession*, this recurrent Christian belief that the end is near. It was, of course, there from the begining, in the self-understanding of Christians, perhaps in the self-understanding of Jesus himself, who nevertheless tells his disciples that neither he as the Son of God nor the Angels of God know "that day and hour" (Matt 24.36). This final ignorance of the end-time brackets all Patrick's statements about it, for he knew his Scripture too well not to have this key text from Matthew always in mind: indeed he twice refers to the chapter in which it occurs. But it seems a fair inference that Patrick was writing in an ambience in which the expectation of the "end" was keen and widespread. Clearly he wanted to make the most of the assumption that the far shores of Ireland coincided with the geographical "World's End", and thus to underline the importance of his own mission and its providential character.

Like many Christian writers from St. Paul onwards, Patrick's inner horizon, by which all facts and observations are put in their place, transcends the visible world of space and time. The *Confession* tells us next to nothing of the social and political reality within which his Irish experiences took place. It is as if nothing really mattered apart from what G. K. Chesterton called "the souls of Christian people." This is not to say that Patrick lacked a sense of community but only that the one community which really mattered to him was the universal community of what came to be called the Communion of Saints, which St. Augustine had called the "City of God." He does indeed distinguish between various nations and tribes, especially in *Coroticus*, and he was indelibly conscious of his own family and social background, yet all this is relativised and absorbed by his sense of the Kingdom and the Gospel of the Kingdom (40). As regards the world of nature and all that belongs to "the warm precincts of this cheerful day" we are faced with the same question in Patrick as in St. Paul: were such things ignored because the writer did not have any real place for them in his heart or only because he was writing about other things? I would hazard the opinion that in both cases, certainly in Patrick's case, there is in the writing itself, in the whole feel of the text, a revealing presence of human pathos and a sense of the fragile beauty of the world we inhabit that gives depth and colour to Patrick's narrative, especially when he is, as it were, taking leave of it all. Here, I think, the image of Pulcherrima has a place, not as overcome or rejected but as given back to that Eternal Beauty from which she has come, and which she so truly radiates in the glow of her baptism.

The *Confession* exemplifies that ever-changing dialectic of heaven and earth, of the beyond and the here and now, which is at the center of Christianity as the acceptance and assimilation of God-with-us, of the Word not *in* the flesh but as *becoming* flesh. This is indeed an uneasy balance, now tipping over into worldliness, now being volatilised into what may be called "celestialism." There is much in Patrick which goes in this latter direction, including his Rule of Faith (4) and his "End" eschatology. Yet for all that, the *Confession* remains an earthed and grounded document, as does also *Coroticus*. It is this quality of natural and human realism that most of all links Patrick with that naturalistic and humanistic quality which was later to distinguish Celtic Christianity from most forms of Catholicism and of Protestant Christianity, both of which have lain and still lie under the shadow of the late Augustine.

10

The Pierced Heart

Any portrait of Patrick, the son of Calpornius, that claims
to be at once historically situated and complete, at least in
outline, must be based firmly and almost exclusively on the
Confession. Almost, but not quite. For Patrick has left us
another document of unquestionable authenticity, that is to
say, unquestionably written by the man who wrote the *Confession*. The *Coroticus* letter is in fact generally taken to
predate the *Confession*, and it is indeed possible that the
trouble stirred up by the incident which occasioned the letter
may have led to the writing of the *Confession*. It seems likely
that the letter which has survived, as an earlier letter of
Patrick's to the same Coroticus did not survive (*Cor* 3), may
have done harm to Coroticus and his friends, and so led to an
attack on Patrick that put him in the position of defendant.

Coroticus was, it seems, a Romano-Briton, a fellow-
countryman of Patrick, a military leader, probably a local
chieftain or king; one ancient source calls him "The King of
Aloo" (*rex Aloo*) identified by present-day scholars as Dum-
barton on the Clyde (Hanson *in loco*). It seems that this
regional chieftain raided the Irish coast and killed and took
captive a group of Christians recently baptised by Patrick and
his priests (*Cor* 3). Patrick mourns those who have been

slaughtered, but he is most agonisingly concerned with those taken captive, "God's servants and the baptised handmaids of Christ," who are being sold as slaves "to the utterly degraded cruel and apostate Picts" (*Cor* 7, 15). And he invokes pertinently and movingly the words of St. Paul, "if one member weeps, let all the members share that grief" (1 Cor 13.26). The letter, addressed as much, if not more, to the followers of Coroticus as to Coroticus himself, is a sustained cry of anguish, almost a cry of despair, as Patrick thinks of the degradation to which these Christians, the women especially, are being subjected. It must be remembered that Patrick is speaking from experience: he knows what it is to be a slave, and he allows himself no words of easy comfort. Christian hope can only cling blindly to the Cross on which Christ is dying (*Cor* 7).

The darkness of the human tragedy which is at the centre of Patrick's letter opens downwards into the deeper darkness of damnation. Coroticus, with those who follow and obey him, is damned. They are all "rebels against Christ," and their lot is "the lake of everlasting fire" of Rev 21.8. In some of his most eloquent passages Patrick contrasts the lot of these "murderers" with the glory that awaits those whom they have murdered. These will reign "with the apostles and prophets and martyrs" (*Cor* 18), while Coroticus and his crew "will be scattered like clouds of smoke in the wind." Yet at the end Patrick holds out the hope of forgiveness, the possibility that "God may inspire them to repent" (*Cor* 21), and try to undo some of the evil they have done. This evil was not only the evil of murder but also the evil of sacrilege, for they have laid violent hands on the Lord's anointed "on whose brows the holy oil of baptism still shines radiantly" (*Cor* 3), "beloved brothers and children newly begotten in Christ" (*Cor* 16).

As a Christian minister Patrick was bound to hold out hope of forgiveness even to the most abandoned sinner, but his offer of reconciliation to Coroticus was essential to the whole purpose of the letter. For the letter came with a very specific request. It is that the *women* captives at least should be released by way of atonement for the great evil that has been done. Again and again it is the lot of the women that pierces

Patrick most deeply, and his great hope is that his letter will have the effect of bringing them back. It seems a forlorn hope, especially as an earlier request of the same kind had been treated with derision (*Cor* 3). It would seem that what Patrick is hoping for is a change of heart on the part of Coroticus in response to a divine inspiration.

It is significant that the letter condemns the actions of Coroticus as sacrilege rather than as murder and enslavement. The kind of raid this local chieftain carried out in an alien land on an alien and barbaric people was an everyday matter at the time, one of the principal ways in which a leader proved and maintained his leadership. Power could be maintained only through the presence of enemies to be overcome. It is doubtful whether Coroticus could have responded to Patrick's appeal without irrecoverable loss of face. Yet as a Christian prince he could not entirely ignore this powerful appeal from a Christian bishop, and it seems not unlikely that Coroticus or his friends dealt with this by challenging Patrick's Christian credentials. If this were the case it is easy to see how the situation which was envisaged in the letter could have developed into the situation envisaged in the *Confession*. By attacking a powerful prince Patrick could have aroused powerful opposition, not only civil but ecclesiastical as well. Indeed it is not unlikely that Patrick's first letter, which Coroticus treated with total contempt, called forth some dismissive references to Patrick and his doings, for in the surviving letter Patrick gives considerable space to a defence of his character and mission. It seems likely enough that the stigma of slavery clung to his name, so that here as in the *Confession* he has to make the point that he was born free and indeed the son of a Roman decurion (*Cor* 10).

Patrick was not only called a Pigman, he was also called an Irishman, a name likely to have been no less disreputable. Even in the fifth century, it would seem, Britain, now Romanised for several centuries, found in its sister island a land and a people to despise. That this contempt has continued to this day (as bearing on Ireland and "the Irish" rather than the individual Irish man or woman) indicates perhaps a deep human need for the presence, in the case of any great nation, of the Despised Other in order to preserve its own image of goodness and greatness. It may well be that this arrogance that even today can call up against it anger and bitterness of Homeric dimensions, is the key to Anglo-Irish relations. This, however, is speculation, whereas the situation that is revealed by Patrick's writings is clear. The Irish are despised by the people from which Patrick came and Patrick is despised with them. *Indignum est illis Hiberionaci summus:* it is a matter of contempt to them that we are Irish (*Cor* 16). Here for a brief moment Patrick is ready to identify himself with his Irish converts, and this is so contrary to Patrick's repeated insistence that he is *not* Irish that commentators are hard put to it to make sense of the statement (see Hanson *in loco*). For it cannot be denied that Patrick was typical of his Romano-British background in his attitude toward the people among whom he suffered the hardships and humiliations of slavery. They are heathens (34) and barbarians (*Cor*) while Patrick makes it clear that he is by birth the son of noble Roman Christian parents (*Cor* 10). This claim to nobility is curiously commemorated in a popular Irish saying which runs half-ironically: "St. Patrick was a gentleman; he came of dacent people."

From the point of view of racial belonging then, Patrick is a divided man, who on the one hand identifies with this people that he has won for Christ at the ends of the earth, and on the other is constantly careful to distance himself from a barbarian people. He has chosen to live among them only because of the divine call so vividly expressed in his dream concerning "the voice of the Irish." Were it not for the bright image of Pulcherrima and the deep and very personal anguish revealed in every paragraph of the *Coroticus* letter, it might be thought that Patrick patronised the Irish and saw them merely as depersonalised "souls to be saved." As it is, all these residual Roman attitudes are cleansed by a great and enduring sorrow, by a cleansing stream that flows from a heart deeply pierced after the manner of the pierced heart of Christ himself. Perhaps this above all, the pierced heart, ever more radiant as ever more deeply pierced, is the most important legacy that Patrick has left to the people whom he served. One can indeed speculate here on the connection across the centuries between this piercing of the heart of Patrick and the acceptance by Irish Christianity in recent centuries of what is called devotion to the Heart of Jesus (usualy connected with the "revelations" of St. Margaret Mary) balanced in more recent times by a similar (though subordinate) Marian devotion. Today this devotional fervour is waning in Ireland as elsewhere, yet it may be asked whether it may not have deep roots in the far Celtic past of Patrick and his inner world, as it has even deeper roots farther back still in the New and Old Testaments.

The most ancient understanding of the pierced heart of Christ centers on the incident of the opening of the side of the Crucified One by the lance of the soldier. The author of the Fourth Gospel presents this incident as extremely significant (19.35), and sees it as the fulfillment of a very moving and mysterious passage from the prophet Zachary: "I will pour out on the house of David and the inhabitants of Jerusalem a spirit of compassion and supplication, so that when they look on him whom they have pierced, they shall mourn for him, as one mourns for an only child, and weep bitterly over him, as one weeps over a firstborn" (12.10). Zachary goes on to speak of wounds received "in the house of my friend," so that the piercing is seen in its inner essence as the result of betrayal. There is here an archetypal situation that renews itself again and again in those who follow the Crucified One all the way, as Patrick desired to do (59). So it is that the experience of the total betrayal of a close friendship is central to the *Confession* as a document revealing, in Bishop Duffy's words, "the roots of a personality."

This betrayal could scarcely be more painful. It was done to him by his special friend (*amicíssimus*) to whom he had in his anxiety confided a sin of his youth, probably no more important than other such sins in almost every life. This his friend brought out into the open when there was question of Patrick's ordination as a bishop for the Irish mission (26, 27). It is easy to hear the self-righteous and poisonous words of this "most dear friend" as he feels "obliged in conscience" to block Patrick's ordination. However the words were spoken,

Patrick never forgot them: the wound is still as fresh and flowing as ever in the heart of the old man who writes his "Confession before I die" (62). There is no bitterness, but there is abundance of grief and pain: it has never ceased to flow in union with the saving streams from the pierced heart of Christ. The wound dealt by Coroticus went very deep, yet not as deep as this. It is in these words most of all that Patrick is a living and eternal image of the Crucified God whom he served.

11

Portrait of a Mystic

1

Mysticism has been understood, and sometimes misunderstood, in a large variety of ways, and there are those who claim that the word should be avoided. Yet the word does name an idea which is a bright star in the intelligible heavens, and the idea identifies and illuminates a set of deep and varied experiences, all of which look towards the Source or Centre of all vision and aspiration.

However, not every experience of the Source counts as mystical, but only experiences of a certain intensity and transforming power. There is the crossing of a threshold, and beyond that threshold a new world and a new life. Above all there is a breakthrough into presence and receptivity, unique, profound, unmistakable. St. Teresa of Avila compares this change to that of a great inundation of life-giving rain falling on the parched earth which up to that point has been painfully irrigated by human labour. In the Fourth Book of her *Interior Castle* she describes this great change or "turn" after which the glories, trials and transformations of mystical, or as she calls it, supernatural, prayer become the daily bread of the soul. This journey into the interior (where God dwells in the seventh or innermost mansions) is described no less powerfully by St. John of the Cross, and these two sixteenth century

Spanish Carmelites have provided an elucidation of Christian mysticism which supplies the structure for all subsequent discussion, though it must be remembered that they were themselves heirs of a tradition of communication with the Source which goes back to the origins of Christianity and beyond, a tradition which may be compared to a great river of many tributaries, some of which flow not only from the world of the Old Testament but from other worlds and other prophets and movements. Only gradually and painfully are we coming to realise the unity of this tradition, which can nevertheless be seen as part of a cosmic mystery centred on the sacrificial death and bodily Resurrection of Jesus of Nazareth.

There are no doubt some Christian authors who either confine the mystical and mysticism within the limits of Christian experience, or else make a sharp distinction between Christian and other mysticisms to the disadvantage of the latter, admitting no commerce between the two kingdoms, one of which is nonetheless dark for being illuminated by phantom lights and inhabited by siren voices. This attitude is of course taken for granted all along the wilder shores of evangelical fundamentalism. This does not really concern me here, but there are some serious and distinguished writers such as Jacques Maritain and R. C. Zaehner who adopt a similar attitude, at least to the extent of refusing to see any real commerce between Christian and non-Christian religious experience. It is an option that goes back to Tertullian and beyond, and it will be always with us. Indeed this attitude is a necessary counterpoise in our day to a facile supermarket approach to religion and the sacred.

Nevertheless it seems to me that this attitude diminishes the divine power and presence in the world. Even if one holds, as I do, that Jesus Christ is the way, the truth and the life (Jn 14.6), and indeed the only way to the Father-Source of our being, yet it is only by seeing the same Jesus in context and in, so to speak, cosmic irradiation, that we see him in his full and unique dimensions. The One who came down from Heaven is, when all is said, no different from Krishna or Osiris if he is not also and equally the One who arises and emerges within the process of universal genesis and of human history, and brings all this involvement and belonging along with him. In our own day we have had this ancient Cosmic Christology opened up to us in contemporary terms by Teilhard de Chardin, and it provides us with the framework we need in order to affirm a mystcal theology at once universal and specifically Christian.[18]

But this kind of approach can become a kind of Christian imperialism, unless we realise that the Christic Centre needs its radii and circumference as truly as they need their unifying centre. Christ needs Buddha and Zarathustra and Pythagoras as well as Plato and Plotinus in order to be fully and gloriously himself: how else can He be seen as the culmination and fulfillment of God's relationship with *all* men and women (Acts 1; Col 1.13-17; 1 Cor 15.28)?

From this point of view the Christian mystic is indeed Christ-centred, and the Christ-centre is the historical Jesus of Nazareth. But Christ is uderstood firstly in the context of the Trinity or Triunity of Father, Son and Holy Spirit, and secondly as in open and reciprocal relationship to the human spirit in all its incarnate depths and vicissitudes. It is within this world that Christian mystical experience emerges as an intensification of an I-Thou prayer relationship where at a certain turning-point God takes over in a transforming expe-

[18]See J. H. Lyons, *The Cosmic Christ in Origen and Teilhard de Chardin*, (Oxford University Press, 1982). There is what may be called a Celtic cosmic consciousness which links together Teilhard (from that part of France, around Clermont-Ferrand, where the Celtic past is still honoured) and Scotus Eriugena in the ninth century, and has a deep connection with the Greek Fathers who were overshadowed for Western Christendom generally by Tertullian and Augustine. I do not think it is fanciful to see this cosmic consciousness as present in Patrick's *Confession*, as it is clearly present in the *Breastplate* and in what has survived of Celtic prayers and practices. See Carmichael's *Carmina Gadelica* (Edinburgh: Oliver and Boyd, 1900-1954), 5 vols. G. R. D. McLean's *Poems of the Western Highlanders* (SPCK, 1961) is an elegant translation of the bulk of Carmichael's collection, but it has been out of print since the early seventies. Still available is a shorter collection of Carmichael's own translation entitled *The Sun Dances* and published by Floris Books of 21 Napier Road, Edinburgh. Only the full Carmichael edition provides the Gaelic originals, with their haunting cadences and their clear witness of a vanished world still full of the living spirit.

rience or series of experiences. No Christian mystic or mystical theologian claims that this kind of experience is essential to "salvation"; it may even be argued that there is another way forward to the higher reaches of Christian commitment and fulfillment, a more ordinary and even pedestrian way. But the mainstream Christian tradition has always allowed mysticism a high, if not the very highest place, among Christian lifestyles, and it would seem that we are witnessing today a new recognition of its legitimacy and its unique importance.

In the context of this new awakening it is important to try to understand not only those authors who are obviously and directly mystical, but also those in whom the mystical current has become obscured because of an emphasis on other aspects of their Christian witness. It is to this class that the author of the *Confession* outstandingly belongs.

2

From our reading of the *Confession* a countenance has emerged, full face and profile. Full face you find the eyes clear and searching and the mouth sensitive and firm; in profile there is an impression of intelligence and far vision. But most of all there is that anointed quality as of a flowing and shimmering radiance that is in some degree, and however faintly at times, the mark of the mystic, the man or woman who has been given to drink abundantly of the Holy Spirit. In this mystical countenance there may indeed be signs of a continuing struggle against the three enemies of the soul — the world, the flesh and the devil — but for all that the inner glow is not quenched. There will certainly be signs of a continuing purification as the mystic is brought deeper into the dark valleys where there is no light at all, and the way forward is indicated only by "the fire that burns in the heart."[19]

---

[19]See the poem *On a Dark Night* and the commentary on it in the Kavanaugh-Rodriguez edition of the Complete Works of St. John of the Cross. I have tried to bring out the significance of this "fire in the heart" in ch. 3 of *Lovelier Than the Dawn*, (Avila, Carmelite Centre of Spirituality, Dublin, 1984).

Patrick wrote the *Confession* not as an account of his spiritual developent as Augustine wrote *his* Confession and Teresa wrote her *Life*. As we have seen, the book is primarily a defence of his mission and an attempt at establishing his missionary credentials. Yet the main lines of Patrick's spiritual development show through, and they are unmistakably the lines of a mystical journey. There is the time of conversion and first favours; there are the later archetypal trials of rejection, betrayal and the sifting of the spirit. There is the opening up of the other side of a man's nature, the feminine, with its tears and tenderness and its enduring strength. Yet there is no resting in this interiority, for Patrick has to face Coroticus and all the responsibilities of his "laborious episcopate" (26). So the feminine and masculine work together in the fragrance of the anointing Spirit, in the mothering and fathering of this great people born anew into Christ "at the ends of earth" (58).

Patrick finds himself in the Heart of Christ through the piercing of his own heart. His whole inner life has its heartbeat in love received and returned. Two words affirm this heartbeat: a word received, *he who has given up his life for you, he it is who speaks in you* (24), and a word freely pledged, *I am ready and indeed yearn with all my heart to receive that chalice to drink which my Lord gives to those he loves* (57). The words are simple and have none of the art of words forged in the smithy of the mind, but they are burning words straight from the furnace of the heart. Indeed the *Confession* can only be rightly read in the glow of that conflagration which is the Heart of Christ.

Patrick would agree with John of the Cross that this inner fire which burns in the heart is to be identified with the Holy Spirit. It is therefore the Spirit of Christ, yet it is also the Spirit of Love which unites the Father and the Son and which has its dwelling place within the human spirit that is receptive to it. This is the central and culminating Christian mystical Source-experience of the Triune Deity, and it shines forth from the depths of the *Confession* and gives it life and warmth. This experience is obscured rather than manifested by the Trinitarian formulae in the Rule of Faith passage (4) and elsewhere, for the experience itself is single and indivisible. It is indeed

correctly and most accurately expressed in the Trinitarian
Formula of Matt 28.19, but the experience itself is deeper
than the intellectual apprehension of the formula. It is in this
sense that we must understand St. Teresa when she tells us
that the mystical journey culminates in an experience of the
Trinity. This experience is related by Teresa as a vision.[20] The
author of the *Confession* has no such vision to relate, yet the
whole book is pervaded by this vision. It is this above all that
he had in his heart to share with the Irish who had asked him
to walk among them (23). It was in the name of this inward
glory that he washed them clean and anointed them in the
ritual of baptism. It was the mystical fire of the Holy Spirit
within him that interpreted the formula of baptism, and drew
a whole people towards the true Sun that threw all the lights
of the old mystique into the shadows (59).

3

Yet as the shadows lose all their partial and preparatory
lightsomeness they merge into the dark, and the dark comes
forward with its own terrible power. This Patrick had to face
again and again, not least in that waking dream of paralysing
terror at the vestibule of sleep, the memory of which never left
him (20). Did he have to face it in all its annihilating terror as
he passed through the doorway of that final sleep? Did it
enclose him in an eternal (seeming) Gethsemane? Perhaps it is
here — in his encounter with final lostness and nothingness —
that Patrick is indeed the warrior-saint of legend and tradition. If he did not banish the snakes from the green fields and
holy hills of Ireland, perhaps he, for all of us, faced the
snake-pit of horror and despair. If he did not fast for forty
days and forty nights on the Western hill that now bears his
name, perhaps he followed his master into the desert to face
the enemy of humankind. If he did not compose that marvel-
lous Breastplate Hymn to which his name is attached, perhaps he had indeed found for all of us the shield to ward off
the attacks of Satan and the advancing gates of Hell.

[20] *Interior Castle* VII. I.

Certainly Patrick had in full measure that mystical strength-in-weakness of which St. Paul speaks (2 Cor 12.10). He knew that this weakness had to be total, that Hope had to be utterly naked in order to face the Adversary, finding its assurance in no inner assurance but only in its own total helplessness (20).

Did Patrick have to face the Nights of Sense and Spirit of which St. John of the Cross speaks? He does not use the kind of terminology that John uses, yet he knew well the texts, mostly from the Old Testment, in terms of which John sets forth this doctrine. Eugene Mullen, the Carmelite poet, in his noble *Ode to St. Patrick* sees the saint as entering the Dark Night of Sense during his slave-years and the far more profound Night of Spirit in his later years.[21] We know that St. John himself saw a deep relationship between the Night of Spirit and that fatherhood of many children which was preeminently the vocation of Patrick. There is indeed a piercing poignancy and totally grounded humility about the *Confession* which might well situate it in the Night of Spirit.

The deeper mystical experience of light and darkness strengthen the soul and spirit without in the least hardening or desensitizing the personality. Rather do they open up or free two fountains deep within, the fountain of tears and the fountain of joy. The sensitive reader of the *Confession* catches the sound of each of them, at different times, or as commingling like the apocalyptic "sound of many waters" (Rev 1.15).

4

The Patricius who wrote the *Confession* and the *Coroticus* letter has sometimes been confused with a certain Palladius, or Patricius Palladius, who was sent to Ireland in 431 by Pope Celestine to deal with what was understood as the Pelagian tendency of the Irish Church. Pelagius had emphasised those aspects of the Christian faith which affirm human freedom and responsibility even in man's fallen state. This was no

[21]See Appendix 2 below.

novelty. Indeed the mainstream Catholic Church in the West has repeatedly affirmed human freedom against the predestinationism and anti-humanism of various breakaway groups. However, Pelagius and his followers found themselves in controversy with the aging St. Augustine, and the teaching Church discovered an *ism* which as such it felt it had to reject, and which it set out to extirpate far and wide. And so we have the mission of Palladius with which our author's mission has been commonly confused, even by those who realise that they were distinct.

There is in fact nothing about Pelagius or Pelagianism in the *Confession* or the *Coroticus* letter. Neither is there any reference to original sin nor any affirmation of an all-pervasive human sinfulness. Patrick is indeed deeply conscious of his own sins and his own great and continuing need of divine assistance. He is also quite forthright in his rejection of paganism and in affirming the need for men and women to be converted to Christ and baptized into a new life. For Patrick, too, the forces of evil are real and powerful, so that there is an absolute and continuous need for the breastplate of Christ's protection. Indeed, as has been said, the celebrated hymn named *St. Patrick's Breastplate* is exactly in tune with the theological tone of the *Confession*.

Again, it is no less difficult to protestanise Patrick than to romanise him. If there is nothing about Rome or a mission from Rome nor indeed the least bow of head or knee in that direction in his writings, neither is there anything about justification by faith or predestination. Some Protestant commentators point to the fact that Patrick cites St. Paul's Epistle to the Romans more frequently than any other Scripture document, and of course Luther rests his case for justification by faith squarely on this central Christian text. But if we look at the index of Scripture references in Hanson's edition we find that Patrick does not have a single reference to that part of the Epistle on which Lutheranism rests (chs 3, 4 and 5); neither does he make any reference to the predestination texts in ch. 9. Indeed a careful examination of Patrick's use of Romans would reveal much not only about Patrick's theology but would serve as an illustration of the thesis of H. G.

Gadamer and others that a text lives most truly in its historical usage and application, and it would leave us with the
question: why did Martin Luther in his time and place read
the text so differently from the way Patrick read it in fifth
century Ireland?

All this bears directly on the mysticism of Patrick. For the
mystic is the man or woman who looks directly at God and
allows the divine light and fire to penetrate the personality at
all levels. For those who feel that they are totally fallen, totally
saturated in sin and guilt, all that can be done is to cling to
Christ in total faith and in the trust that his righteousness will
serve to cover human iniquity in its awful and irredeemable
nakedness. "I have found my personal Saviour, and so God
sees me no longer but Christ who covers me." For the mystic,
on the other hand, all is open, nothing is covered up. What
Christ does through his Holy Spirit is to cleanse and burnish
the Divine Image in me which has been clouded over or even
deeply corroded by original and personal sin. One does not
have to dismiss the thesis of "justification by faith alone," or
deny its grandeur or liberating power for those to whom it
speaks, to see that it does not easily open that direct face-to-
face mystical dialogue with God which, I would claim, is basic
to the *Confession* of Patrick.

Great men illuminate, and few men have so illuminated our
Christian consciousness as St. Augustine who begins his *Confession* by saying *Thou hast made us for Thyself, O Lord* (ad
te: *unto thyself) and our hearts are restless until we rest in
Thee*, and who brings this mighty hymn of praise to its
conclusion with the invocation of the "beauty forever ancient
and forever new." He is indeed one of the great beacons or
lighthouses of Christian history, and his light guides us on-
ward still and warns us of rocks and shallows. But great men
sometimes (perhaps always) cast great shadows, and the pes-
simism and anti-humanism of the later Augustine has cast a
chilling gloom across Western Christendom. Only Celtic
Christianity has entirely escaped this shadow. In this tradition
men and women have opened to God and have trusted human
nature in each other. Men and women have also opened to
nature, to the earth and sea and sky. This is clearly expressed

in a stanza of *St. Patrick's Breastplate* sometimes omitted.
Here it is in Mrs. Alexander's vigorous translation:

> I bind unto myself to-day
> The virtues of the star-lit heaven,
> The glorious sun's life-giving ray,
> The whiteness of the moon at even,
> The flashing of the lightning free,
> The whirling wind's tempestuous shocks,
> The stable earth, the deep salt sea
> Around the old eternal rocks.[22]

This Celtic nature-theology is most richly and powerfully
expressed in that unique monument of ancient Christian
witness and consciousness, Alexander Carmichael's *Carmina
Gadelica* with its subtle and imaginative recognition of the
divine presence and the heavenly presences in the ordinary
events and rhythms of life, from the kindling of the fire on the
hearth in the morning to the smooring of the same fire at
night, and the lying-down invocations to the Trinity and
Mary and the Angels and Paul and Patrick himself. For
Patrick's great and childlike spirit lives on in the hidden days
and ways of the many generations of his children.

---

[22]St. Patrick's Breastplate (Latin: *lorica* Gaelicised as *liureach*) is traditionally
attributed to Patrick himself. This attribution cannot be proved, yet neither can it be
totally disproved. The hymn is written in Old Irish, and this goes back to Patrick's
time and can indeed boast of being the earliest European vernacular literature. See
Myles Dillon, *Early Irish Literature* (University of Chicago Press, 1948) p. xvi and
passim. The *Breastplate* is a protection prayer of the kind very common in the Celtic
tradition as is clear from the *Carmina Gadelica* (Note 18, above). The legend is that
by the singing of it Patrick and his companions appeared to their enemies as herd of
deer — hence the hymn is also called "The Deer's Cry" (*Faeth Fiada*). The original is
to be found in *Thesaurus Palaeohibernicus* (Stokes-Strachan, 1903). See *A Golden
Treasury of Irish Poetry* by David Greene and Frank O'Connor, (Macmillan, 1967);
also see P. C. Henry's *Shoithuileachtna Sean-Ghaeilge* (Government Publications,
Dublin, 1978). Professor Henry writes (I translate): "The early stanzas are very
Christian, very orthodox. But the fourth stanza has the feel of the ancient pre-
Christian religion, and is concerned with the nature and power of the elements" (p.
137). There are many English translations of the *Breastplate* including one by James
Clarence Mangan, and it has been several times set to music. Yet it is on the whole
neglected by our churches, as if it brought with it an atmosphere, not unacceptable
certainly, but somehow other or alien.

Select Bibliography

L. Bieler, *Libri Epistolarum Sti Patricii*, Dublin: Irish Manuscripts Commisstion, 1952. This is the generally accepted scholarly edition of the original Latin texts of the *Confession* and *Coroticus*.

Binchy, D.A., "Patrick and His Biographers, Ancient and Modern," *Studia Hibernica* 2 (1962), 7-173.

Bury, J.B., *Life of St. Patrick*, London, 1905. An elegantly written book, still readable, though not always reliable.

Carney, J., *The Problem of St. Patrick*, Dublin, 1961. Deals with some scholarly questions and disagreements.

Chadwick, Nora, *The Celts*, Penguin Books, 1970 (1984). At once scholarly and readable this provides the general pre-historical and historical background of Celtic Christianity.

Corish, P.J., *The Irish Catholic Experience*, (Wilmington, Delaware: Michael Glazier, Inc., 1985).

Dillon, Myles, *Early Irish Literature*, Chicago, 1948 (1969). This provides the background of Patrick's writings from a literary standpoint.

Duffy, Joseph, *Patrick in his own Words*, Dublin: Veritas Publications, 1975. The Bieler text with an English translation and notes.

Hanson, R.P.C., *Saint Patrick: Confession et Lettre á Coroticus*. Avec la Collaboration de Cécile Blanc. Editions du Cerf: Paris, 1978. (Sources Chrétiennes, No. 249). This very complete edition, with exhaustive indices, is the essential *instrument de travail* of Patrician study today.

——————— *The Life and Writings of the Historical St. Patrick*, New York: The Seabury Press, 1983. The English presentation of Patrick's writings has a full introduction, which must stand as the best contemporary English life of Patrick. This edition omits the textual apparatus of the French book, and also the indices.

——————— *Saint Patrick, His Origins and Career*, Oxford, 1968.

Hood, A.B.E. (ed. and tr.), *St. Patrick, His Writings and Muirchu's Life*, London and Chichester, 1978.

Hughes, K. *The Church in Early Irish Society*, London, 1966.

O'Brien, J.F.X., S.J. *The Confession of St. Patrick*, Dublin: Irish Messenger, 1924. This careful and readable translation based on the Newport White text (1918) is still easily and cheaply available. It contains Sigerson's excellent translation of Patrick's *Lorica*.

O'Donoghue, N.D., *The Spirituality of St. Patrick* in *Studies*, Summer 1961.

O'Driscoll, R. (ed.), *The Celtic Consciousness*, Canongate: Edinburgh, 1981. Based on the papers read at a conference on Celtic History, Art and Literature in 1978, this large, beautiful and expensive book places our author and his writing within what the editor calls "the Celtic continuum."

Ryan, J., *St. Patrick, Apostle of Ireland*, in *Studies* (Dublin) Vol. L, no. 198, Summer 1961.

Ryan, John, *Irish Monasticism*, Dublin, 1931. This is still the most complete account of the monastic background of St. Patrick and Celtic Christianity.

Wright, Charles H.H., *The Writings of St. Patrick*, Religious Tract Society: London, 1889. This nineteenth century translation of the *Confession* and *Coroticus* was a work of scholarship in its own time, but obviously it has been superseded by later scholarly editions of the Latin text. However, it has not in my opinion been superseded in literary quality. It is as clear and sharp as the original, and also flows very pleasantly and readably. It is now out of copyright as well as being long out of print, and I have chosen it as a reference text for the present book, it being understood that for deeper study the reader should go to the Bieler or Hanson editions. It should be noted also that Wright's Scriptural references, though interesting are not exhaustive nor always accurate: For Patrick's use of Scripture, Hanson's (French or English) editions should be consulted.

Appendices

Appendix A
The Confession of Patrick
Translated by C.H.H. Wright

1 I Patrick, a sinner, the rudest and the least of all the faithful, and most contemptible to very many, had for my father Calpornius, a deacon, a son of Potitus a presbyter, who dwelt in the village of Bannavem Taberniae, for he had a small farm hard by the place where I was taken captive. I was then nearly sixteen years of age. I did not know the true God; and I was taken to Ireland in captivity with so many thousand men, in accordance with our deserts, because we departed from God, and we kept not His precepts, and were not obedient to our priests, who admonished us for our salvation. And the Lord brought down upon us 'the wrath of His indignation,' (2 Chron. 29. 10) and dispersed us among many nations, even to the end of the earth, where now my littleness is seen among foreigners.

2 And there the Lord opened (to me) the sense of my unbelief, that, though late, I might remember my sins, and that I might return with my whole heart to the Lord my God, who had respect to my humiliation, and pitied my youth and ignorance, and took care of me before I knew Him, and before I had wisdom, or could discern between good and evil; and protected me and comforted me as a father does a son.

102 Appendix A - The Confession of Patrick

3 Wherefore I cannot keep silent — nor is it indeed expedient (to do so) — concerning such great benefits, and such great favour as the Lord has vouchsafed to me in the land of my captivity; because this is our recompense (to Him) that, after our chastening, or knowledge of God, we should exalt and confess His wonderful works (Psa. 107. 15) before every nation which is under the whole heaven.

4 Because there is no other God, neither ever was, neither before, nor shall be hereafter, except God the Father, unbegotten, without beginning. From whom is all beginning; upholding all things, as we have said; and His Son Jesus Christ, whom indeed with the Father, we testify to have always been, before the origin of the world, spiritually with the Father; in an inexplicable manner begotten before all beginning; and by Himself were made the things visible and invisible; and was made man; (and), death having been vanquished, was received into the heavens to the Father. (Rev. 3. 21) And He has given to Him all power 'above every name of those that are in heaven, on earth, and under the earth, that every tongue should confess' (Phil. 2. 9-11) to Him that Jesus Christ is Lord and God, in whom we believe, and expect (His) coming, to be ere long 'the Judge of the living and of the dead,' (Acts 10. 42) 'who will render to every one according to his deeds.' (Rom. 2. 6) And he hath 'poured upon us abundantly' (Titus 3. 6) the Holy Spirit, a gift and pledge of immortality; who makes the faithful and obedient to become 'sons of God, and joint-heirs with Christ;' (Rom. 8. 17) whom we confess and adore — one God in the Holy Trinity of the Sacred name.

5 For He Himself has said by the prophet, 'Call upon Me in the day of thy tribulation, and I will deliver thee, and thou shalt magnify me.' (Psa. 1.15) And again He saith, 'It is honourable to reveal and confess the works of God.' (Tobit 12. 7)

6 Although I am in many respects imperfect, I wish my brethren and acquaintances to know my disposition, and that they may be able to comprehend the wish of my soul.

7 I am not ignorant of the testimony of my Lord, who witnesses in the Psalm, 'Thou shalt destroy those that speak a lie.' (Psa. 5. 6) And again, 'The mouth that belieth killeth the soul.' (Wisdom 1.11) And the same Lord says in the Gospel, 'The idle word that men shall speak, they shall render an account for it in the day of judgement.' (Matt. 12. 36)

8 Therefore, I ought earnestly with fear and trembling to dread this sentence in that day when no one shall be able to withdraw himself, or to hide, but when we all together shall render account of even the smallest of our sins before the tribunal of the Lord Christ.

9 Wherefore, I thought of writing long ago, but hesitated even till now; because I feared falling into the tongue of men; because I have not learned like others who have drunk in, in the best manner, both law and sacred literature in both ways equally; and have never changed their language from infancy, but have always added more to its perfection. For our language and speech is translated into a foreign tongue. As can be easily proved from the drivel of my writing — how I have not been instructed and learned in diction; because the wise man says: 'For by the tongue is discerned understanding and knowledge, and the teaching of truth.' (Ecclus. 4. 29)

10 But what avails an excuse (although) according to truth, especially when accompanied with presumption? Since indeed I myself, now in my old age, strive after what I did not learn in my youth, because they prevented me from learning thoroughly that which I had read through before. But who believes me, although I should say as I have already said? When a youth, nay almost a boy in words, I was taken captive, before I knew what I ought to seek, or what I ought to aim at, or what I ought to avoid. Hence I blush to-day, and greatly fear to expose my unskilfulness, because, not being eloquent, I cannot express myself with clearness and brevity, nor even as the spirit moves, and the mind and endowed understanding point out.

11 But if it had been granted to me even as to others, I would not, however, be silent, because of the recompense.

And if, perhaps, it appears to some, that I put myself forward in this matter with my ignorance and slower tongue, it is, however, written: 'Stammering tongues shall learn quickly to speak peace.' (Isa. 32. 4) How much more ought we to aim at this — we who are the 'epistle of Christ' — for salvation even to the end of the earth, (Acts 13. 47) — and if not eloquent, yet powerful and very strong — written in your hearts 'not with ink,' it is testified, . . . 'but by the Spirit of the living God.' (2 Cor. 3. 3) And again the Spirit testifies; 'and rusticity was ordained by the Most High.' (Ecclus. 7. 15)

12 Therefore, I, first a rustic, a fugitive, unlearned, indeed, not knowing how to provide for the future — but I know this most certainly, that before I was humbled I was like a stone lying in deep mud; and He who is mighty came, and in His own mercy raised me, and lifted me up, and placed me on the top of the wall. (Comp. 1 Peter 2.5; Eph. 2. 21, 22) And hence I ought loudly to cry out, to return also something to the Lord for His so great benefits, here and in eternity, which benefits the mind of men cannot estimate.

13 But, therefore, be ye astonished, both great and small, who fear God. And ye rhetoricians, who do not know the Lord, hear and examine: Who aroused me, a fool, from the midst of those who appear to be wise, and skilled in the laws, and powerful in speech and in every matter? And me — who am detested by this world — He has inspired me beyond others (if indeed I be such), but on condition that with fear and reverence, and without complaining, I should faithfully serve the nation — to which the love of Christ has transferred me, and given me for my life — if I should be worthy — that, in fine, I should serve them with humility and in truth.

14 In the measure, therefore, of the faith (Rom. 12. 3) of the Trinity it behoves me to distinguish, without shrinking from danger, to make known the gift of God, and His 'everlasting consolation,' (2 Thess. 2. 16) and without fear to spread faithfully everywhere the name of God, in order that even after my death I may leave it as a bequest to my brethren, and to my sons, whom I have baptized in the Lord — so many thousand men.

15 And I was not worthy nor deserving that the Lord should grant this to His servant; that after going through afflictions and so many difficulties, after captivity, after many years, He should grant me so great favour among that nation, which when I was yet in my youth I never hoped for, nor thought of.

16 But after I had come to Ireland I daily used to feed cattle, and I prayed frequently during the day ; the love of God and the fear of Him increased more and more, and faith became stronger, and the spirit was stirred; so that in one day I said about a hundred prayers, and in the night nearly the same; so that I used even to remain in the woods and in the mountain; before daylight I used to rise to prayer, through snow, through frost, through rain, and felt no harm; nor was there any slothfulness in me, as I now perceive, because the spirit was then fervent within me.

17 And there indeed one night, in my sleep, I heard a voice saying to me, 'Thou fastest well (fasting so), thou shalt soon go to thy country.' And again, after a very short time, I heard a response saying to me, 'Behold, thy ship is ready.' And it was not near, but perhaps two hundred miles away, and I never had been there, nor was I acquainted with any of the men there. After this I took flight, and left the man with whom I had been six years; and I came in the strength of the Lord, who directed my way for good; and I feared nothing till I arrived at that ship.

18 And on that same day on which I arrived, the ship moved out of its place, and I asked them (the sailors) that I might go away and sail with them. And it displeased the captain, and he answered sharply with indignation, 'Do not by any means seek to go with us.' And when I heard this, I separated myself from them in order to go to the hut where I lodged. And on the way I began to pray; and before I had ended my prayer I heard one of them, and he was calling loudly after me, 'Come quickly, for these men are calling you.' And immediately I returned to them, and they began to say to me, 'Come, for we receive you in good faith, make friendship with us in whatever way you wish.' And in that day I accord-

ingly disdained to make friendship with them, on account of the fear of God. But in very deed I hoped of them that they would come into the faith of Jesus Christ, because they were heathen, and on account of this I clave to them. And we sailed immediately.

19 After three days we reached land, and for twenty-eight days we made our journey through a desert. And food failed them, and hunger prevailed over them. And one day the captain began to say to me, 'What (is it), O Christian? You say thy God is great and almighty; why, therefore, canst thou not pray for us, for we are perishing with hunger? For it will be a difficult matter for us ever again to see any human being.' But I said to them plainly, 'Turn with faith to the Lord my God, to whom nothing is impossible, that He may send food this day for us in your path, even till you are satisfied, for it abounds everywhere with Him.' And God assisting, it so came to pass. Behold, a herd of swine appeared in the path before our eyes, and (my companions) killed many of them, and remained there two nights, much refreshed. And their dogs were filled, for many of them had fainted and were left half-dead along the way. And after that they gave the greatest thanks to God, and I was honoured in their eyes. From that day forth they had food in abundance. They also found wild honey, and offered me a part of it. And one of them said, 'It has been offered in sacrifice.' Thanks be to God! I consequently tasted none of it.

20 But the same night while I was sleeping, and Satan greatly tempted me, in a way which I shall remember as long as I am in this body. And he fell upon me like a huge rock, and I had no power in my limbs, save that it came to me, into my mind, that I should call out 'Helias.' And in that moment I saw the sun rise in the heaven; and while I was crying out 'Helias' with all my might, behold the splendour of that sun fell upon me, and at once removed the weight from me. And I believe I was aided by Christ my Lord, and His Spirit was then crying out for me, and I hope likewise that it will be thus in the days of my oppression, as the Lord says in the Gospel, 'It is not you that speak, but the Spirit of your Father, which speaketh in you.' (Matt. 10. 20)

21 And again, after many years, I was taken captive once more. On that first night, therefore, I remained with them. But I heard a Divine response saying to me, 'But for two months thou shalt be with them'; which accordingly came to pass. On that sixtieth night the Lord delivered me out of their hands.

22 Even on our journey He provided for us food and fire, and dry weather every day, till on the fourteenth day we all arrived. As I stated before, we pursued our journey for twenty-eight days through the desert, and the very night on which we all arrived we had no food left.

23 And again, after a few years, I was in the Britains with my parents, who received me as a son, and earnestly brought me that, now at least, after the many hardships I had endured, I would never leave them again. And then I saw, indeed, in the bosom of the night, a man coming as it were from Ireland, Victoricus by name, with innumerable letters, and he gave one of them to me. And I read the beginning of the letter, containing 'The Voice of the Irish.' And while I was reading aloud the beginning of the letter, I myself thought indeed in my mind that I heard the voice of those who were near the wood of Foclut, which is close by the Western Sea. And they cried out thus as if with one voice, 'We entreat thee, holy youth, that thou come, and henceforth walk among us.' And I was deeply moved in heart, and could read no further; and so I awoke. Thanks be to God, that after very many years the Lord granted to them according to their cry!

24 And on another night, I know not, God knows, whether in me, or near me, with most eloquent words which I heard, and could not understand, except at the end of the speech one spoke as follows, 'He who gave his life for thee (1 John 3. 16) is He who speaks in thee;' and so I awoke full of joy.

25 And again I saw Him praying in me, and He was as it were within my body, and I heard him above me, that is, above the inner man, and there He was praying mightily with groanings. And meanwhile I was stupefied and astonished, and pondered who it could be that was praying in me. But at

the end of the prayer He spoke as if He were the Spirit. And so I awoke, and remembered that the Apostle says, 'The Spirit helps the infirmities of our prayers. For we know not what we should pray for as we ought; but the Spirit Himself asketh for us with unspeakable groanings,'(Rom. 8. 26) which cannot be expressed in words. And again, (he says) 'The Lord is our advocate, and prays for us.' (1 John 2.1; Rom. 8.34)

26 (And when I was attacked by some of my seniors, who came and (urged) my sins against my laborious episcopate, so that on that day I was strongly driven to fall away, here and for ever. But the Lord spared a proselyte and stranger for His name's sake. He kindly and mightily aided me in his treading-under, because in the stain and disgrace I did not come out badly. I pray God that it be not reckoned to them as an occasion of sin.

27 For after thirty years they found me, and brought against me a word which I had confessed before I was a deacon. Under anxiety, with a troubled mind, I told my most intimate friend what I had one day done in my boyhood, nay in one hour; because I was not then used to overcome. I know not, God knows, whether I was then fifteen years of age; and I did not believe in the living God from my infancy; but I remained in death and unbelief until I was severely chastised; and in truth I have been humbled by hunger and nakedness, and that daily.

28 On the other hand, I did not of my own accord go to Ireland until I was almost worn out. But this was rather good for me; for by this I was corrected by the Lord — and He fitted me that I should be today what formerly was far from me; that I should be filled with care, and be concerned for the salvation of others; since at that time I did not think even about myself.

29 Then in that day on which I was reproached for the things above-mentioned; on that night, I saw in a vision of the night, a writing against me, without honour. And at the same time I heard a response saying to me, 'We have seen with displeasure the face of the designate with his name stripped.' He did not say, 'You have seen with displeasure,' but 'We have

seen with displeasure,' as if He had joined Himself to me, as He has said, 'He that toucheth you is as he that toucheth the apple of Mine eye.' (Zech. 2. 8)

30 Therefore I gave thanks to Him, who comforted me in all things, that He did not hinder me from the journey on which I had resolved, and also from my work which I had learned of Christ my Lord. But the more from that (time) I felt in myself no little power, and my faith was approved before God and men.

31 But on this account I boldly assert that my conscience does not reprove me now or for the future. 'God is my witness' (Rom. 1. 9; comp. Gal. 1. 20; 2 Cor. 1. 23) that I have not lied in the statements I have made to you.

32 But I am the more sorry for my very dear friend — to whom I trusted even my life — that we should have deserved to hear such a response. And I ascertained from several brethren before that defence that, when I was not present, nor in Britain, nor did it originate with me — even he in my absence made a fight for me. Even he had said to me with his own mouth, 'Behold, thou art to be promoted to the rank of bishop,' — of which I was not worthy. But whence then did it occur to him afterwards that before all, good and bad, he should publicly put discredit upon me, although he had before of his own accord gladly conceded (that honour to me)? It is the Lord, who is greater than all.

33 I have said enough. But, however, I ought not to hide the gift of God which He bestowed upon us in the land of my captivity. For then I earnestly sought Him, and there I found Him, and He preserved me from all iniquities, so I believe, because of His Spirit 'that dwelleth in (me),' (Rom 8. 11) which has wrought in me again boldly even to this day. But God knows, if a man had spoken this to me, I might have been silent for the love of Christ.

34 Wherefore, I give unwearied thanks to my God, who has kept me faithful in the day of my temptation; so that I may to-day confidently offer to Him my soul — to Christ my Lord

— as a sacrifice, 'a living victim; (Rom. 12. 1) who saved me from all my difficulties,' (Psa. 34. 7) that I may say: 'Who am I, Lord?' (2 Sam. 7. 18) and what is my vocation, (1 Cor. 1. 26.) that to me Thou hast co-operated by such Divine grace with me! So that to-day I can constantly rejoice among the Gentiles and magnify (Rom. 15. 9) Thy name wherever I may be, not only in prosperity, but also in distresses; (2 Cor. 12. 9, 10) that whatever may happen to me, whether good or evil, I ought to receive it equally, and always to give thanks to God, who has shown me that I should believe in Him, the indubitable one, without ceasing, and that He will hear me; and that I, though ignorant, may in these last days attempt to approach this work, so pious and so wonderful; that I may imitate some of those of whom before the Lord long ago predicted (that they) should preach His Gospel, 'for a testimony to all nations' (Matt. 24. 14) before the end of the world. Which, therefore, has been so fulfilled, as we have seen. Behold, we are witnesses that the Gospel has been preached everywhere, in places where there is no man beyond.

35 But it would be long to relate all my labour, in details, or even in part. Briefly, I may tell how the most holy God often delivered me from slavery, and from twelve dangers by which my life was imperilled, besides many snares, and things which I cannot express in words, neither would I give trouble to my readers. But there is God the Author (of all), who knew all things before they came to pass. (So, however, the Divine response very frequently admonished me His poor pupil.

36 Whence (came) this wisdom to me, which was not in me, I who neither knew the number of my days, (Psa. 39. 4) nor was acquainted with God? Whence (came) to me afterwards the gift so great, so beneficial, to know God, or to love Him, that I should leave country and parents.

37 And many gifts which were offered to me with weeping and tears? And, moreover, I offended against my wish certain of my seniors. But, God overruling, I by no means consented or complied with them. It was not my grace, (1 Cor. 15. 10) but God who conquered in me, and resisted them all; so that I

came to the Irish peoples, to preach the Gospel, and to suffer insults from unbelievers; that I should listen to reproach about my wandering, and (endure) many persecutions, even to chains; and that I should give up my noble birth for the benefit of others. And if I be worthy, I am ready to lay down my life unhesitatingly, and most gladly for His name; and there I wish to spend it, even till death, if the Lord permit.

38 For I am greatly a debtor to the God who has bestowed on me such grace, that many people through me should be born again to God, and that everywhere clergy should be ordained for a people newly coming to the faith, whom the Lord took from the ends of the earth, as He had promised of old by His prophets: 'To Thee the Gentiles will come and say, As our fathers made false idols, and there is no profit in them.' (Jer. 16. 19) And again: 'I have set Thee to be the light of the Gentiles, that Thou mayest be for salvation unto the utmost part of the earth.' (Acts 13. 47; Isa. 49. 6)

39 And there I am willing to wait the promise of Him who never fails, as He promises in the Gospel: 'They shall come from the east and the west, and shall sit down with Abraham, and Isaac, and Jacob;' (Matt. 8. 11) as we believe that believers shall come from all the world.

40 Therefore it becomes us to fish well and diligently, as the Lord premonishes and teaches, saying: 'Come ye after me, and I will make you fishers of men.' (Matt. 4. 19) And again He says by the prophets: 'Behold I send many fishers and hunters, saith the Lord.' (Jer. 16. 16) Therefore it is very necessary to spread our nets, so that a copious multitude and crowd may be taken for God, and that everywhere there may be clergy, who shall baptize and exhort a people needy and anxious, as the Lord admonishes and teaches in the Gospel, saying: 'Going, therefore, teach ye all nations, baptizing them in the name of the Father, and of the Son, and of the Holy Spirit, ... even to the end of the age.' (Matt. 28. 19) And again: 'Going, therefore, into the whole world, preach the Gospel to every creature. He that believeth and is baptized shall be saved, but he that believeth not shall be condemned.' (Mark 16. 15, 16) And again: 'This Gospel of

the kingdom shall be preached in the whole world, for a testimony to all nations, and then shall the consummation come.' (Matt. 24. 14) And also the Lord, foretelling by the prophet, says: 'And it shall be in the last days, saith the Lord, I will pour out of my Spirit upon all flesh, and your sons and your daughters shall prophesy, and your sons shall see visions, and your old men shall dream deams. And upon My servants indeed and upon My handmaids I will pour out in those days of My Spirit, and they shall prophesy.' (Acts 2. 17, 18; Joel 2. 28, 29) And in Osee He says: 'I will call that which was not My people My people . . . and her who had not obtained mercy; and it shall be in the place where it was said, You are not My people, there they shall be called the sons of the living God.' (Hosea 1.9, 10; Rom. 9. 25, 26)

41 Whence, then, has it come to pass that in Ireland they who never had any knowledge, and until now have only worshipped idols and unclean things, have lately become a people of the Lord, and are called the sons of God? Sons of the Scots and daughters of chieftains are seen to be monks and virgins of Christ.

42 And there was even one blessed Scottic maiden, nobly-born, very beautiful, of adult age, whom I baptized. And after a few days she came to us for a reason, and intimated to us that she had received a response from a messenger of God, and he advised her that she should be a virgin of Christ, and that she should draw near to God. Thanks be to God! On the sixth day after that, she most excellently and eagerly seized on that which also all the virgins of God do; not with the will of their fathers — but they suffer persecution and false reproaches from their parents; and notwithstanding the number increases the more; and of our own race who were born there (there are those), we know not the number, besides widows and those who are continent. But those (women) who are detained in slavery especially suffer; in spite of terrors and threats, they have assiduously persevered. But the Lord gave grace to many of my handmaids, for, although they are forbidden, they zealously imitated Him.

43 Wherefore, though I could wish to leave them, and had been most willingly prepared to proceed to the Britains, as to my country and parents; and not that only, but even (to go) as far as to the Gauls, to visit the brethren and to see the face of the saints of my Lord. God knows that I greatly desired it. But I am 'bound in the Spirit,' (Acts 20. 22) who 'witnesseth to me,' (Acts 20. 23) that if I should do this, He would hold me guilty; and I fear to lose the labour which I have commenced; and not I, but Christ the Lord, who commanded me to come, and be with them for the rest of my life. If the Lord will, (James 4. 15) and if He will keep me from every evil way, (2 Tim. 4. 18; comp. Gen. 28, 20) that I may not sin before Him.

44 But I hope (to do) that which I ought; but I trust not myself, so long as I am in 'this body of death; (Rom. 7. 24) for strong is he who daily tries to subvert me from the faith, and from the chastity of religion proposed (to myself), not feignedly (which I will observe), even to the end of my life, to Christ my Lord. But the flesh, which is in enmity, (Rom. 8. 7) always leads to death, that is, to unlawful desires to be unlawfully gratified. And I know in part that I have not led a perfect life, as other believers. But I confess to my Lord, and I do not blush before Him, because I lie not: from the time that I knew Him in my youth, the love of God and His fear have increased in me; and until now, by the favour of the Lord, 'I have kept the faith.' (2 Tim. 4. 8)

45 Let him who will laugh and insult, I will not be silent, nor will I hide the signs and wonders which were ministered to me by the Lord, many years before they came to pass, as He who knew all things even before the world began. (Acts 15. 18)

46 But hence I ought to give thanks without ceasing to God, (Comp. 1 Thess. 5. 17, 18) who often pardoned my ignorance (and) my negligence, even out of place, not in one instance only — so that He was not fiercely angry with me, as being one who was permitted to be his helper. And yet I did not immediately yield to what was pointed out to me,

and (to) what the Spirit suggested. And the Lord had pity on me among thousands of thousands, because He saw in me that I was ready, but that in my case for these (reasons) I knew not what to do about my position; because many were hindering this mission, and already were talking among themselves, and saying behind my back, 'Why does that fellow put himself into danger among enemies who know not God?' Not (as though they spoke) for the sake of malice, but because it was not a wise thing in their opinion, as I myself also testify, on account of my defect in learning. And I did not readily recognize the grace that was then in me; but now I know that I ought before (to have been obedient to God calling me).

47 Now, therefore, I have related simply, to my brethren and fellow-servants who have believed me, (the reason) why I have preached and do preach, in order to strengthen and confirm your faith. Would that you might aim at greater, and perform mightier things! This will be my glory, because 'a wise son is the glory of a father.' (Prov. 10. 1; Prov. 15. 20)

48 You know, and God also, how I have conducted myself among you from my youth, both in the faith of the truth, and in sincerity of heart. (1 Thess. 2. 10) Even in the case of those nations among whom I dwell, I have always kept faith with them, and I will keep it. God knows I have overreached none of them; neither do I think of it, (that is, of acting thus) on account of God and His Church, lest I should excite persecution against them and us all, and lest through me the name of the Lord should be blasphemed; because it is written, 'Woe to the man through whom the name of the Lord is blasphemed.' (Lev. 24. 16; Rom. 2. 24)

49 For though I am unskilful in names, yet I have endeavoured in some respects to serve even my Christian brethren, and the virgins of Christ, and religious women, who have given to me small voluntary gifts, and have cast off some of their ornaments upon the altar; and I used to return these to them; although they were offended with me because I did so. But I (did it) for the hope of eternal life, in

order to keep myself prudently in everything, so that the unbelieving may not catch me on any pretext, or the ministry of my service; and that, even in the smallest point, I might not give the unbelievers an occasion to defame or depreciate me.

50 But perhaps, since I have baptized so many thousand men, I might have expected half a screpall from some of them? Tell it to me, and I will restore it to you. (1 Sam. 12. 3) Or when the Lord ordained everywhere clergy, through my humble ministry, I dispensed the rite gratuitously. If I asked of any of them even the price of my shoe, tell it against me, and I will restore you more.

51 I spent for you, that they might receive me; and among you, and everywhere, I travelled for your sake, amid many perils, even to remote places, where there was no one beyond, and where no one else had ever penetrated — to baptize or ordain clergy, or to confirm the people. The Lord granting it, I diligently and most cheerfully, for your salvation, defrayed all things.

52 During this time I gave presents to the kings; besides which I gave pay to their sons who escorted me; and nevertheless they seized me, together with my companions. And on that day they eagerly desired to kill me; but the time had not yet come. (John 8. 20) And they seized all things that they found with us, and they also bound me with iron. And on the fourteenth day the Lord set me free from their power; and whatever was ours was restored to us for God's sake, and the attached friends whom we had before provided.

53 But you know how much I paid to those who acted as judges throughout all the regions which I more frequently visited. For I think that I distributed among them not less than the hire of fifteen men. So that you might enjoy me, and I may always enjoy you in the Lord, I do not regret it, or is it enough for me — I still 'spend, and will spend for your

souls.') God is mighty, and may He grant to me that in future I may spend myself for your souls.

54 Behold, 'I call God to witness upon my soul' (2 Cor. 1. 23) 'that I lie not; (Gal. 1. 20) neither that you may have occasion, nor because I hope for honour from any man. Sufficient to me is honour which is not belied.

55 But I see that now I am exalted by the Lord above measure (2 Cor. 12. 7) in the present age; and I was not worthy, nor deserving that He should aid me in this; since I know that poverty and calamity suit me better than riches and luxuries. But Christ the Lord was poor for us. (2 Cor. 8. 9) But I, poor and miserable, even if I wished for riches, yet have them not, 'neither do I judge my own self;' (1 Cor. 4. 3) because I daily expect either murder, or to be circumvented, or to be reduced to slavery, or mishap of some kind. (But 'I fear none of these things,' (Rev. 2. 10) on account of the promises of the heavens; for I have cast myself into the hands of the Omnipotent God, who rules everywhere, as saith the prophet, 'Cast thy thought on the Lord, and He will sustain thee.' (Psa. 55. 22)

56 Behold now, I commend my soul to my most faithful God, (1 Pet. 4. 19) for whom I discharge an embassage in my ignoble condition, because indeed He does not accept the person, (Gal. 2. 6; Prov. 18 5) and He chose me to this office, that I might be one of the least of His ministers.

57 But 'what shall I render Him for all the things that He hath rendered to me? (Psa. 116. 12) But what shall I say, or what shall I promise to my Lord? Because I have no power, unless He had given it to me, but He searches 'the heart and reins;' (Psa. 7. 9; Jer. 11. 20) because I desire enough and too much, and am prepared that He should give me 'to drink of His cup,' as He has granted to others that love Him. (Matt. 20. 22, 23)

58 Wherefore may it never happen to me from my Lord, to lose His people, (people) whom He has gained in the

utmost parts of the earth. I pray God that He may give me perseverance, and count me worthy to render myself a faithful witness to Him, even till my departure, on account of my God.

59 And if I have ever imitated anything good on account of my God, whom I love, I pray Him to grant me, that with those proselytes and captives, I may pour out my blood for His name's sake, even although I myself may even be deprived of burial, and my corpse most miserably be torn limb from limb by dogs, or by wild beasts, or that the fowls of heaven should devour it. I believe most certainly that if this should happen to me, I shall have gained both soul and body. Because without any doubt we shall rise in that day in the brightness of the sun, that is, in the glory of Jesus Christ, our Redeemer, as 'sons of the living God,' (Hosea 1. 10) and 'joint-heirs with Christ,' (Rom. 8. 17) and to be 'conformable to His image; (Rom. 8. 29) for 'of Him, and through Him, and in Him' (Rom. 11. 36) we shall reign.

60 For that sun which we behold, at God's command, rises daily for us — but it shall never reign, nor shall its splendour continue; but all even that worship it, miserable beings, shall wretchedly come to punishment. But we who believe in and adore the true sun, Jesus Christ, who will never perish; neither shall he 'who does His will,' — but 'shall continue for ever,' (1 John 2. 17) — as Christ continues for ever, who reigns with God the Father Almighty, and with the Holy Spirit, before the ages, and now, and through all the ages of ages. Amen.

61 Behold, I will, again and again, declare briefly the words of my Confession. I testify in truth, and in joy of heart, before God and His holy angels, (1 Tim. 5. 21) that I never had any reason, except the Gospel and its promises, for ever returning to that people from whom I had formerly escaped with difficulty.

62 But I beg of those who believe and fear God, whoever shall deign to look into or receive this writing, which Patrick the sinner, unlearned indeed, has written in Ireland, that no

one may ever say, if I have done or demonstrated anything according to the will of God, however little, that it was my ignorance (which did it). But judge ye, and let it be most truly believed, that it has been the gift of God. And this is my Confession before I die.

Appendix B
Ode to St. Patrick
by Eugene Mullen

ST. PATRICK! — name that breaketh as siren song
Filling the cavernous aisle of the past, and wooeth
The untrammelled heart with mem'ry of far-spent tide
That bore unto our sea-caressed coast
High-laden argosy from Celestine:—

GREAT Patrick, three full cycles have rolled their span
And marked in the maze the tireless troll of time
Since thou to Erin sailedst. Upon the wide
Domain of Caesar's lands darkness, an age,
Has brooded: chastisement condign invoked
To nourish cleansing in voluptuous Romans.
Thus, passion purged in Chaos' crucible,
The Vandal midnight pall to matin twilight
Was resolved before the rising sun of Peter;
And guided by his voice, in semi-darkness
Men walked, a second age, in rude simplicity.
Its trinal path the ample orb of Time
Pursuing, morning blushed for waking man.
Renewed the ancient face of earth beneath
Aurora's smile. Renewed, alas, withal,
The pristine pride that made man's greatness folly.
Ere long, impatient of the Trusted Guide,

He missed the way, and wandered in confusion.
Thou, shrouded in glory, hast not felt the irksome
Cavalcade of time; yet mirrored in the face
Of God, we know not how, thou must have seen
These ages, year by year, teem with the golden
Harvest of thy sowing.

THREE Cycles, a far horizon for the mind
To scan; but as, with wistful eyes we thither
Turn us, thy lordly figure looms transcendent;
And walking through the days in majesty,
Trails high destiny. In Columban and St. Gall
In the night it walks, a lamp to all the world
Of sanctity and lore. Thy task fulfilled,
It knows, withal, the twilight of eclipse,
When ruined shrines are tongues to speak thy shrunken
Memory. Yet, now, not filial faithlessness
But trial of adversity thy form
Obscures, dimming thy lustre. Awhile, and thou
Shalt see another Nero, shalt unearth
Another Catacomb. To tarnish thee,
Nurtured in Wisdom's strong caress of pain,
Aurora's godless grace availeth not.
And as, when the Scourge of God the limbs of Europe
Mangled, thou gavest house and healing, so,
'Mid the dread disintegration of the millions
Thou standest by Loyola's side and great
Teresa's, portentous bulwark, undemolished,
Undiminished, bruised yet still unseamed,
A ridge of rock unrent. And from thy woes
Emerging Atlantean, thou sufferest
A grave dispersion of thy flock to leaven
Weaker folds...
        To-day the great recall:
A Foclut in the east is musical;
And thou art with thy children once again:
At the Banquet of the Eucharist, the dear,
Sweet, honoured guest: to every mind instinct
With Faith, and heart aglow with Ireland's love —
A form palpable and a power felt!

O Prince of light, thou glory of our race!
In gentle mien desired of serf and sage;
In vast dominion, Source of Erin's greatness;
In bloodless conquest whole, Apostle peerless;
In thy festival, the exile's link with home;
In thy missionary sons, beloved of Rome;
In thy mountain prayer, our animating hope
That ne'er that fire shall have been built in vain
That flamed defiance from the hill of Slaine!

As over thy dead body Ireland watched,
Nor darkness on thy face allowed to fall
Throughout the length of twelve obsequial days,
So to thy living spirit we overt
Obeisance make and homage pay with all
The congregated fervour of our race!

AND while, with hearts dilated, we contemplate
Thy apostolic name, the eager mind
Would know what deeps of life pulsating lie
Beneath the cosmic tide of influence
That from thee ebbless flows. The answer lies
In thine own words on thy captivity:
But then it was the love of God began
To grow within me. Not to the Apostle but
The slave, exiled from kindred, race and tongue;
Nay, even from the foreigner apart,
Incarcerated in an open dungeon
There to consume his term of days and nights
In utter loneliness of soul, go we
To sound those privy deeps and glimpse afar
The abysmal womb whence issued all thy greatness.

In this dark night of sense was born in thee
That aching void that groaneth invitation
Unto the cloudless solitude of God.
Thenceforward Lady Charity, with coy
And distant mien, looked sweet upon thee; thenceforth
Castilian lance she couched to front the foe
In thee; the while by hidden ways, as thou
Couldst travel, with soft names numberless called thee.

And swiftly thou didst run to her embrace,
A hundred times a day and in the night.
Gradually from the breasts of tenderness she weaned
Thine infant mouth, and bade thee grow in love
Upon the food of pain. She gave thee snow
To be thy raiment, and for thy home a shed;
Till, stripped of carnal ease, thy spirit glowed
In strength of love. . . .
　　　　Yet many seasons still
Remained before the term of thy lengthy trial
Was closed. More inward now the workings
Of thine all-comely Consort; pure spiritual
Even unto that region mute whence springs
All nobleness in man. Can human vision
Vainglorious pierce the ray of darkness fallen
On that holy, silent place within thee, and speak
Thy soul's espousals, these hapless happy days?
Dire agony thrills the marrow when the Bridegroom
Godhead enters, the sunlight of His Face
Nigh marring mortal eye; and much divine
Inflowing thou received: celestial flood
To inundate, and make thee sweet and willing.

THEN to His chosen one the Master spoke:
　　"Arise and go: thy ship awaits thee
　　On the western main." Ended thy servitude,
Bondsman, a nobler service to begin:
The land that held thee slave to win for Christ!
With vision dim of that exalted calling,
To the soldier-saint of Tours thou turnedst thy footsteps,
To drink of sacred learning from his lips.
Thence to Germanus, sapient and holy,
Who taught thee wisdom, that gracious quality
Of lordly minds that guides and sanctifies
All knowledge. Lastly to Honoratus didst
Thou go: Meet Paradise for angel envoys
Chanting to thee the innocents' wail inspired:
Come, Patrick; come, and walk once more with us.

WHAT joy filled Heaven when on our verdant soil
Thy blessed feet their eager print impressed
To mark the way of Truth revealed in Christ!
Now fronting Darkness' Powers stood such an one
As might have stirred the martial Spirit, Michael.
In strongest citadel with panoply
He faced the foe, and deadly issue joined.
No more would Druid altar smoke; no more
Belial; Christ for ever more: the Mass.
But while thou overturnedst their gods of stone,
Thou approvedst their cultured ways and on the old
Foundation raised a grander edifice.
Whithersoe'er thou camest all hearts thou didst
Beguile. In thee the nation viewed with awe
That matchless one whom they could make their chief:
Brave, wise and fair as written in the code.
At Tara, Duffach, first of Erin's Seers,
Arose to honour thee against a king's
Command; Benignus sweetly broke thy sleep
To speak his love unto thy breast with blossomed
Strewings. And as thou faredst upon thy way
The lovely princess daughters of the west
Found charm in thy address and saving unction
Nay more, the men of science knelt to thee,
And brought their art and showed it unto thee;
And all the poets and the men of law,
That thou mightest know the judgments of true nature
Spoken by the wise before thou camest hither.
These scattered sheaves gleaned from the golden fields
Of patriarchal vision thou with care
Didst garner and winnow unto Christ; the Bardic
Strain from banquet song to hymnal didst
Resolve; the fierce cacaphony of hate
Attune unto the euphony of love.

AND as, in the fullness of the world's time,
To the new-found race of olden dereliction
Seraphic Paul proclaimed the sanctions
Of the law, so thou to judges and to kings

The canons of integrity and virtue
Didst declare. "Fear not man but God, O judge,"
Thou saidst, "and take not gifts, for these blind judgment.
Know justice and with prudence speak, so judging
As you look for judgment. And thou, O king,
Be just, with mercy; protect the stranger and
The widow; exalt not wicked men, but choose
The wise and upright as thy counsellors;
To Druids lend no countenance, but faith
Profess and pray unto thy God with sober
Brow. Thus fruitful trees shall find the land
And gentle winds shall blow, and peace be as a river."

TO all the seven kingdoms thou didst go
With toilsome journeyings, in sore privation.
Armagh thy See Primatial thou didst make,
God's angel guiding. On the Willow Ridge
By that proud hill, which Macha, golden-haired
With aureate pin had lined to trace the site
Of Eamhain Fort and shape a home of valour
For the bold Craobh Ruadh, thy pastoral staff now marked
The place of more enduring battlement.
"Great glory this last House shall have" said the Lord
Of Hosts "and in this place I will give thee peace."
To kindly Cineal Eoghain thou didst grant
Wide sovereignty, wielded from fair Aileach.
Of Munster's zealous sons thou wert beloved,
Who wept to see thee gone. At Cashel Aongus
Gladdened thee with a royal "Yea" of faith
And won thy blessing upon this home of Kings.
At Tailte, heroes strove to win the bays
And from thy hand the higher guerdon took
Of living waters. Thence to the glamorous west
Thou turnedst, where thou didst catch, forsooth, the wistful
Witchery that hath estranged the soul of Eire
And made her heart intransigent; to a land
Where fat fields fail and lovely lakes lie curled
'Neath mirrored hills, sharing, in thriftless joy,
Great Nature's artless remnant; to a people weaned

From the nursling milk of earth's abundance, unquiet
Hunger in their eyes pleading for manna new.
QUIVERED thine arm as Crom thou laidest low?
Leaped thine impassioned soul in premonition
Of myriad love-victims, as thou scarfedst the eyes
Death-lidded of the fair and ruddy daughters?
And didst thou start, and view with kindling eye
That sea-girt mountain-peak that yonder stood,
A shapely sentinel o'er trackless waters,
On the rim of the world? Forsooth thou didst perceive
The living poesy that sheltered in
Those hills, and its kinship close with prayer, divine.
Prayer and poetry, puissant royalties,
Heaved from the mute recess that generates
Beneath the touch of the Most High, his bedesmen
Doth each, in his own kind, with each endue
With vision sheer and with immortal longings!
But when, dear Saint, on houseless hilltop far,
Thy penitential heart was moved in prayer,
Vision prophetic was to thee vouchsafed
And desire as wide and deep as sempiternal.
Thy mansioned soul was swept with halcyon draught
Of glory yet to be. Nay e'en the secret
Centre where Being holds, an open oriel
Is now become, which searchless inspiration
Enfilades. The meaning of the past thou seest
And what the far-flung future holds. Alone
Upon the heights, in this undying hour
Thou art the centre of the universe,
Fast-girdled with zones diurnal of filial love
To come, which burst into an over-widening
Amphitheatre of flame to ease thine high,
High ecstasy. And heaven looking down
Capitulates; and Lady Charity,
Hot valour's minion, enters, captor meek,
Arena cosmic, the plighted troth to take
Of one sweet Sainted Isle, the daughter fair
Of Roland heart of mystic chivalry!

DEAR Motherland, thy sacred face is changed,
The blithesome aspect lost which then It wore
When to thy Paradisal Spouse in wondrous
Mansuetude Thou borest a heavenly brood!
As oil poured out were these Thine hallowed days.
Glory was Greece, in mind and body fair;
But greater glory Thou; for unto Christ,
Not Venus, Thy sapience administered,
And Thine abundant milk. Lured by Thy greeting,
Poor princess came and Thou with Wisdom's gold
Enrichedst them. Alfred Thou didst educate
To Greatness' dizzy height and Alcuin give
To Charlemagne. A social fabric Thou
Didst weave of purer web than aught the world
Has seen. In thy Banquet-hall the King sat with
The Ollamh and the Bard; and in Thy cloister
Bard and Ollamh were courtiers of a Saint;
A Paradise at home, an Empire from
Iona to St. Gall didst Thou create
And raise to amaranthine glory upon
A rock foundation; — Aristocracy
Of Soul.

THE day of Thine illumination
Ended, the bosom of Thy peace was gored,
And Thou wert cast into exterior gloom:
The arid waste and wilderness of spirit,
Where Thou wert fire-tried through long sojourn.
Deep now the lines that furrow Thy once radiant
Brow; inscrutable and deep the pool
Of personality that lies beneath.
Three Cycles Thou hast known of noble striving,
The ferment in Thy blood inspired aye:
Or for Thy Faith, or for Thy Fatherland,
Or both. Who, then, would know Thee must contemplate
That past in living flesh enthroned. Who would
Be true to Thee must regal be, and this
Imperishable witness bear: *Not thus*

Has He chosen every race. O Motherland
Of mighty palpitation, the life Thou hast
To-day, in soul and sense, is, drop by drop,
Pressed from the passionate heart of the past: a cup
Inebriate, for valiant men to taste!

Index